A Tale of Two Turtles

*My True Story as an Incest Survivor
and my Incredibly Amazing
Path to Healing*

Suzanne Souvent

A Tale of Two Turtles: My True Story as an Incest Survivor, and my Incredibly Amazing Path to Healing

Paperback ISBN: 979-8-218-68403-7
Ebook ISBN: 979-8-218-68404-4
Printed in the United States of America

No part of this manuscript is fiction. Some names of people and places have been changed.

Book cover art and design, formatting:
Illumination Graphics

The energies of the past creep unbidden
into the present,
and that is why we must, from time to time,
whether we like it or not,
bring them out, dust them off
and deal with them.

— Suzanne Souvent

Contents

Dedication

To my three beautiful sisters,
whom I will always love.

Acknowledgments

I wish to thank my precious sons who have motivated me, filling my life with joy and meaning.

I also wish to express my deepest gratitude to my steadfast and loving husband who taught me to laugh when I felt like crying and who carried me through life for an entire year; to my dear friend, Judy D., for proofreading my book and then telling me that she enjoyed my story so much that she read it twice, and who, along with my wonderfully supportive friends, Kathy H. and Judi U., made me realize that the shame isn't mine; and to my determined friend, Doretta W., who simply wouldn't let me give up on this book.

Prologue

Full disclosure: I don't actually want to write this book. You'll see why. It's not a pretty story and it's not easy to do. Two compelling reasons oblige me to do so. First, it's just possible that my story might help someone else successfully navigate a similarly tragic circumstance.

And secondly, and more importantly, you see, I don't just "believe" or "have faith in" the unseen hands. I know for certain that they do exist. What happened to me proves this beyond the shadow of a doubt. Amazing but true! There are unseen forces at work, and I and those who know my story have no other explanation for what I am about to share.

Chapter 1

JEKYLL AND HYDE

I loved my father. He adored clowning around and making my sisters and me laugh. He had a way of unexpectedly distorting his face and coming at me that at first startled me, but when I saw him shaking his head back and forth (making his whole face quiver) and then, emitting this low growl, I howled with laughter as he would grab me and affectionately tickle me.

As far back as I can remember, and for no medically discernible reason, my left ear from time to time would ache horribly. At those times, my father would pick me up and set me in his lap. He would gently blow warm cigarette smoke right into that ear until it felt better. Much to my amazement and relief, the painful earache would always stop due to the warmth of his smoke. What a deep feeling of relief and gratitude I experienced when he lovingly made that pain melt away.

Back then, during the 1950s, it was a wonderful time to be a small child. It was a time when Mother often repeated her favorite saying — "the best thing since sliced bread" — which she indeed believed was THE greatest invention of man. She applied this saying to many newly available modern conveniences such as black and white television sets, jet engines, transistor radios, hula hoops, Sputnik, and power steering in automobiles that lacked today's confining seat belts.

No seat belts in cars meant that one lucky child could stand in the middle of the back seat, comfortably leaning into and holding onto the front seat, totally savoring the ride and feeling like she was road surfing!! Not only was it comfortable to both lean and hold on at the same time, but that child — me, when it was my turn — stood in the very center of the vehicle, enjoying a fantastic panoramic view.

Standing there, I felt as if I were actually flying at exhilarating speeds. Fortunately, my father was an excellent driver who enjoyed taking the family out on nice, long Sunday drives, out of the city and into the country — sometimes with me standing up in the back seat for the scenic journey.

I very much loved my father. And I know that, in his own way, he loved me and my sisters. But I detested his beer. Today, more than six decades later, I still can't stand the smell of beer.

My father truly possessed a Jekyll and Hyde personality. When he was drinking, he became violent, terrifying, and unpredictable. The next morning when he awoke, hung over, his jagged cruelty and meanness were unparalleled as he sought out wee victims to inflict misery upon. At the worst times, Mother and us girls literally feared for our lives, and rightly so.

Yet, when sober (and not hung over), Father possessed creative, imaginative, fun-loving and amazing ideas. He stood as the more vibrant of our two parents and I savored those rare moments of joy with him. Mother never really seemed like she was all there, emotionally.

She rarely laughed at his amusing antics like we did. While physically present, she just wasn't quite engaged in the deeper ways that really mattered — the loving, laughing and wildly wonderful ways. In my eyes, Father remained the more adventurous and imaginative one. He was passionate and fully alive, in both positive and negative ways.

Chapter 2

THE "HIGH MAN"

As I awoke, moonbeams coming through the window revealed a ceiling that was once newly painted and bright but now showed cracks in the paint and numerous smudges of dirt. I quietly slipped out of my warm bed, bare feet alighting on a cold, hard, wooden floor. I tiptoed to the staircase, careful as always to make the least amount of noise as possible.

My parents' frequent late-night quarrels had long ago quashed any quick dashing down the long stairs to get to the bathroom. Despite a full bladder demanding to be emptied, angry voices from downstairs and my fears trapped me at the top of the steep wooden staircase. As the bickering drifted up the dark staircase, I hesitated, and cold terror mercilessly jolted me from a half-asleep state into full alertness.

Only four years old, I wore a threadbare nightgown that showed faded brown teddy bears on fabric that once kept me warm, but now only revealed the bones of my skinny body. As with the majority of my clothes, it was a hand-me-down. That same nightgown had warmed my oldest sister, Jackie, and then, my second sister, Karen, but by now didn't have much thread left to keep me very warm at all. And so, I shivered.

On this night as on so many others, I'd been awakened by the need to tinkle, but this time, my tiny bladder was threatening to burst. Even so, I hesitated at the top of the staircase, a pause mandated by fear of my violent father. Thumb in mouth my only comfort, I nervously twirled my long, sandy-colored hair with my free hand and stared at the dark staircase leading to the downstairs. The steps before me were squeaky and unforgiving, and I knew that I had to try to descend without making a sound.

Now fully awake, I considered the journey. I needed to go down the staircase, around the corner to the left at the bottom, over the threadbare carpet in the living room, through the hall, and finally into the small bathroom that was located uncomfortably close to my parents' bedroom. It seemed an impossibly long path, but my bladder gave me no choice.

The staircase stood dead center in the small house. At the bottom and to the right, the large dining room housed not only the dining room table and chairs but also an infant changing table pushed against the far wall. It was utilized for my baby sister, who was now several months old. From that room, the angry shouts emerged.

I cautiously began descending the staircase, testing each step carefully for squeaks. The stench of beer wafted up the staircase, another warning that I must descend ever so quietly. I was terrified of being discovered and becoming the focus of my father's fury. Below, the shouts intensified. As I drew nearer, I could hear their conversation. "It's GOT to stop, Carl!"

"You're exaggerating, Lisa. You know, you're overreacting again."

"I'm not overreacting, Carl! You're hurting the three older girls. You've been hurting them — and it's GOT to stop. Or else!"

"Or else? Or else what? Who's gonna make me stop? You?"

I heard my father's bone-chilling laugh. Using that loud laugh as cover, I quickly stepped down onto the last step and thus hid its well-known creak. I braced myself and then hesitated, afraid to dart out into the open to round the corner into the living room. I cautiously peeked out, hoping that their backs were turned towards me.

"Well, thank God," Mother said, "at least you can't hurt THIS one."

My mother set aside a soiled diaper and caressed my baby sister as she fussed on the changing table.

Mother's back was indeed turned towards me, but her body blocked my view of the baby. Although I could hear Jenna's coos and smell that diaper in the heat of the night, I couldn't see my baby sister. Father was also standing, turned sidewise. Since his back wasn't turned towards me, the fear of discovery glued me to the spot. Mother softly repeated her one comforting thought aloud:

"At least you can't hurt THIS one!"

"Oh, yeah?" my father thundered. "YOU don't tell me what I can and can't do!"

Father roughly pushed Mother aside, and now, his body blocked my view of what was happening. My parents struggled and shouted, but I could not fully see nor understand what was occurring. They shoved each other and yelled. Then, the baby screamed!

Soon after, Mother screamed!

I knew that whatever had happened was horrible, and I stood on that last step, held in place in an almost hypnotic manner. Still undetected, I was affixed to the spot, a desperation to understand what had just happened now overshadowing my fear for my safety.

I stepped down off the last step, hoping to see. Standing silently, I forgot to hide, now in full view of my parents whose backs were turned to me. Out in the open, my full bladder forgotten, I no longer feared for myself but for my beloved baby sister. As painful cries arose from her, I felt as though I was detaching from myself. I experienced a strange sense of calm as I felt myself rising above the chaotic scene, and from that higher viewpoint, saw a tiny trickle of blood on the baby's foot. Finally, the struggling between my parents stopped and Father sat down, victorious and spent.

"There!" he shouted. "No broad tells ME what I can and can't do!"

Mother bent over, half leaning on the changing table, and half bending over it in defeat. At the same time, she tried to calm Jenna. My mother's words took on a startling depth of both tone and content.

"Oh, my God, Carl!! What? Look at what you have done! She's bleeding. Oh, no! Carl, you've broken her *hymen*!" (He had cruelly raped my infant sister with his finger.)

To me, it sounded like Mother had said the word "high man." I'd never heard the phrase "high man" before, and it confused me. Mother's harsh tone of voice made me think it was something very serious. A sickening fear for my baby sister began washing over me, totally overriding the terror I'd been feeling for myself.

Father jumped up, went over to the table, and then sat back down, slowly sinking into the chair. Moaning in despair, he buried his face in his large hands.

"Oh, my God!" he cried. "What have we done!?"

Mother stiffened and swung around, turning her body to face him, and as she next spoke, her words rang strong and distinct, icy and harsh.

"What do you mean 'we' — 'what have WE done'? This was done by YOU, not ME!"

For the first time, and not without a start, Mother saw me out of the corner of her eye and with a shock realized that they were not alone.

"Carl, look!!"

Then he saw me, standing utterly still, literally frozen to the spot. I was afraid to breathe, afraid to run, and afraid to move. I'd been standing there at the bottom of the staircase, hoping that somehow, I had become invisible.

"Susie!! I wonder how long she's been there!"

"Long enough, it looks like," Mother said.

Father exploded from his chair and once again pounced and grabbed me. He put his fingers over my nose, pinching it, and put his hand over my mouth, smothering me, suffocating me. In his drunken terror, he wanted to — no, he needed to — eliminate the innocent witness to the act. HIS evil act.

As I was blacking out, the stench of beer on his breath assaulted and sickened me. Mother, yelling and pulling at him, tried to free me as I slipped into oblivion.

Moments or minutes passed, and slowly, I returned to consciousness. Mother's words and her arms surrounded and comforted me.

"Thank God!" she said. "She's coming around. I think she's alright. Thank God! Oh, she stinks. She's wet herself. She's soaked! Just look at this other mess that you've created, Carl!"

Mother's tone shifted to one of disgust as she proceeded to remove the wet clothing. My full bladder had emptied itself as I had lost consciousness, drenching me with my pee. Although Mother remained livid with her drunken husband's horrific act, she unleashed the wrath she felt towards him not upon him but where it was safer to vent her anger — upon me. An outpouring of disgusted words about the wet pajamas followed as she carried cold, naked me upstairs for fresh ones. The sting of her anger not only deepened my fear, but also added to my sense of confusion and shame. As she carried me upstairs, I was wondering what a "high man" was, and how it could be broken. So I innocently asked:

"Mommy, what's a high man?"

"A hymen, uh, a high man is what YOUR father is when he is drunk. But not high in a good way."

"But how could he have broken Jenna's high man? That doesn't make sense. Besides, she's a girl."

"Shush. That's not something for good little girls to worry about."

Not bothering to wash me or wipe me down in any way, she threw a clean nightgown on me and pushed me towards my bed without any reassuring hugs or kisses, still ignoring my questions. Mother had a crying baby and a broken, sobbing drunk to contend with downstairs. She had no time, energy, nor compassion for stinky, traumatized me. After that night, I stayed in my bed, extremely terrified to risk getting up and venturing downstairs when nature called. So, I began to regularly wet the bed. My sisters eventually took to teasing me about the bed wetting, running from me and taunting, "Peetail! Peetail!"

In addition to everything else, I had now become a Peetail.

Chapter 3

LOVING ACTS

In our family, we three older girls became close, having been born one year after the other. Before us, Mother had had several miscarriages and then, she gave birth to a baby every year for three years in a row: first Jacqueline (affectionately called "Jackie" by pretty much everyone), then Karen, and then me, Susie. Four years after me, Jenna came into this world.

And so, Mother had her hands full, with more than one of us in diapers at a time for several years. Extremely busy, she encouraged my two older sisters to largely look after and take care of me as soon as they were able to. Whenever I fell, it was not Mother who would run over and comfort me, but my oldest sister, Jackie, and she would even get the bandage to cover my scratch. It seemed to me that Jackie, a very caring, loving, smart and energetic sister, loved nurturing both Karen and me.

When snow fell outside, not Mother but Jackie would tell us to get our coats, hats and gloves, and she made sure that they were donned and fastened correctly. She took her sisterly responsibilities seriously, and both Karen and I grew to look up to her.

All three of us girls became athletic. Jackie and I earned the description of tomboys. Although a year older than Karen, Jackie was several inches shorter than Karen. But somehow Jackie's voice, posture, and actions made her appear taller than Karen. Unlike Karen's, Jackie's dark chocolate hair was wildly curly and thick. She had a melodic voice, an adventurous and fearless spirit, and beautiful big blue eyes. Jackie carried herself in a lofty manner, her head held high, proud and unashamed, and ready for the spotlight at any time. She craved attention and got it. During this era of the young actress Shirley Temple, my sister wanted to and indeed did shine.

Karen, with her long, straight, tawny hair, stood tall and slender. Always feeling too tall for her age, she felt that she stuck out unnaturally. As a result, feeling awkward and easily embarrassed, she sought to escape any and all attention. Jackie, of course, who was just the opposite, sought out the limelight, which suited Karen just perfectly, allowing her to shy away from it. In my eyes, Karen was a kind and delicate, quiet but deeply loving sister.

Much that she imparted to me reflected wisdom beyond her years. She taught me the importance of considering another's feelings, and that showing love could never ever be wrong. Karen taught me to treat others the way that I would like to be treated. She taught me kindness, compassion, and empathy.

On the rare occasion when she would utter an angry word, Karen almost immediately followed it up with words of apology and an explanation as to why she had said the angry words in the first place. Extremely sensitive to others' feelings, she couldn't bear to hurt another. And she usually managed to slip out of sight and hide whenever our parents fought.

Karen tried to do everything with a spirit of love, and I respected and adored her for it. Sometimes, when Jackie didn't want me tagging along on an outdoor adventure that she and Karen were setting out on, Karen would rise to my defense and insist that I be allowed to come along. And so, I often tagged along for the outdoor fun.

I loved doing kind, unexpected acts to make my sisters and Mother smile. One morning, I tiptoed into Mother's bedroom, intending to do a good deed. My mother and sisters were still sitting at the kitchen table, finishing breakfast, so I knew if I hurried, I'd have enough time.

Mother and Father's bedroom was small by today's standards with a tall, dark brown clothes dresser to the left as you entered and a small clothes cupboard next to the dresser. The bed took up most of the room with its headboard against an outer wall of the house. At the foot of the bed sat a longer, low dresser which had a mirror mounted on the back. It seemed gigantic to me, and dark and beautiful, with a mirror that was too high to show my tiny reflection. The colorful area rug on the floor, though thin, proved a luxury to walk on, since most of the rest of the house had no rugs. The living room also had an old, dingy thin rug in the middle.

In comparison to the rest of the bedroom, the double bed seemed enormous and also proved a little high for me to reach. I did the best that I could, smoothing out the warm spread, placing and tucking in the pillows, and quickly making the bed. From a very young age, my mother had taught my two sisters and me all the household chores that she possibly could. We washed dishes, swept, straightened up, and scrubbed floors. She taught us that cleanliness mattered a great deal, and I have always felt grateful for that lesson.

I slipped back into the kitchen and sat down with a happy smile on my face, waiting. Eventually, Mother finished her breakfast and walked into her room intending to make her bed.

I, of course, followed closely at her heels, bursting with anticipation. I was not disappointed. She rewarded me with a surprised and joyful, "Oh, my! How lovely! Susie, did you make this bed?"

My soul soared as I confessed to the deed, and

I absorbed her words of praise and gratitude, luxuriating in her ensuing hug. I had put a smile on my mother's face, not an easy thing to do!

On another morning, I again left the kitchen table early with the intent of sneaking into my oldest sister's bedroom and making her bed, hoping to make her smile, too. At the top of the stairs, two small, dormer bedrooms lay tucked under the slanted roof, one of which I shared with my sister, Karen, and the other of which my oldest sister, Jackie, had all to herself. Her room was to the left of the stairs and though there was no door on either bedroom, the stairs provided a divider. Each bedroom also had a small window at the end, providing a little ventilation. The rooms contained no fans, no area rugs on the floors, and were small and stark in comparison to our parents' bedroom. No mirrors hung anywhere, and no pictures graced the walls upstairs.

We were poor, and we knew it. Jackie had a small dresser for her clothes but no clothes closet, the same as Karen and me. Jackie had a little wooden chair in her room, upon which sat a baby doll that Santa had brought. She loved that doll, naming it "Dolly" and fussed with it often, changing Dolly's clothes, rocking her lovingly, and talking to her like she was a real baby. A cheery "Good Morning, Dolly" could often be heard coming from Jackie's bedroom.

On this particular morning, Dolly was still in Jackie's bed, so I carefully picked her up, straightened out her dress, patted down her hair, and placed her in a sitting position in the chair. The window was open, and a delicious breeze filled the often-hot room. I gently told Dolly to please be quiet so that no one would know that I was making Jackie's bed as a surprise for her. After all, my fun lay largely in not being discovered doing a "good deed" as Mother had dubbed them. I finished my quest and ran back downstairs.

I listened from the living room as Jackie climbed that long staircase. She dressed and emerged from her bedroom a short time later, coming back downstairs. With a smile on her face and love in her eyes, she hugged me and said that it had been a wonderful surprise, finding her bed already made. She knew, without asking, that I had made it for her.

And so, in that moment and others like it, I found joy and happiness. Acts like these helped me form a few positive passions at a rather young age. I knew the great joys of giving, of sharing, of laughing together, working together and playing together, thanks to my awesome sisters! I looked up to both of my two older sisters and, in many instances, tried to follow their lead.

My sisters and I spent as much time as we could outside, playing in the sunshine with each other and often with our neighborhood friends. Like children everywhere, we were perpetual balls of energy, jumping rope, playing tag, exploring the neighborhood, enjoying the summer sunshine, and moving at a frenetic pace from the moment our eyes opened in the morning until we curled up into balls in our beds at night. My two older sisters were at times beacons of light and of love, and I followed their lead whenever I could, happy to be in the shadow of their limelight. I learned a lot from both of my older sisters about getting along with others.

Chapter 4

JOHNNY OVER THE OCEAN

We three older sisters were excellent rope jumpers. We could jump rope for hours, taking turns at twirling the rope ends. Jumping rope constituted hours and hours of our outdoor fun. Three was the perfect number of girls needed for rope jumping fun, two girls to twirl the rope and one girl to jump.

Johnny over the Ocean was one of our favorite chants:

Johnny over the Ocean,
Johnny over the Sea
Johnny broke a milk bottle
Blamed it on me
How many lickins did he get?
One — two — three — four — five — six — seven . . .

We three girls were very grateful that we didn't have any nasty little brothers like "Johnny" who might do bad things and then try to blame those naughty deeds on us. We often gave him hundreds of "lickins!"

Most summer mornings, we'd get up, eat our cereal, make our beds, and get out of the house to play before Father woke up, grouchy and often hung over. One particularly warm summer day, we got out early and jumped rope on the street in front of our house all morning long in the warm sunshine.

Mother called us in for lunch. After lunch, we were so anxious to get outside that I ate half of my dessert and then shoved the rest of it (a Hershey's chocolate bar) into my pocket as we ran outside again. We immediately noticed some of neighborhood kids gathering down the street. Joining them, we heard one of the older boys suggest that we all head down to the woods at the end of the street below our street to swing on the monkey vines. Knowing we weren't really allowed to go that far but figuring no one would ever know, we three sisters braved following the group of kids down the street, heading towards adventure.

A steep cement staircase (with a rusted iron railing) led down into the ravine containing the woods – the "wild woods" we called them. Trying to keep up with the older kids, I carefully held onto the railing as I descended the precipitous steps and set foot in the wild woods for the first time! Excited,

I felt it was worth the risk. Besides, with my two sisters along, I felt pretty safe.

A rutted, dirt path led deeper and deeper into the woods, and we three girls tagged along a little way behind the others. Karen suggested that we pretend to be wild horses, and she and I hung back even more and then galloped along the path until we came upon a tall tree nestled deep in the woods, sporting deep green leaves and a few smaller monkey vines. On this beautiful day, those vines weren't the first thing to grasp my attention. I became captivated by tiny droplets of water nestling in the tree. Perfectly bathed in that moment of sunshine, the droplets of dew shimmered from the leaves more brightly than the lights on a Christmas tree! A feeling of magical enchantment enveloped me. Karen went on ahead. I paused, captured by the moment.

As I lingered, my fingers found the precious last piece of chocolate in my pocket, and I brought it out. Then, I noticed a little squirrel climbing down this magical tree. I got an idea. I only had that one piece of chocolate left. Slowly walking towards the squirrel, I held it out in front of me, as an offering. To my utter delight, that tiny creature scampered right up to me, took the chocolate out of my fingers, and began eating it! I had the amazing experience of coming into really close contact with the squirrel and sharing with him the last of my delicious chocolate. Then, he ran away.

I began jumping up and down with excitement over coming so close to that adorable and trusting squirrel. He ran away, but not before those magical moments etched themselves forever in my heart and mind. I ran and caught up with Karen and excitedly told her that I'd given my last piece of chocolate to a little squirrel who ate it right in front of me. She listened politely and gave me a skeptical look.

"Do you expect me to believe that you gave your last piece of chocolate to a SQUIRREL!!!???"

"Yes, I really did! Honestly! I know it sounds crazy, but I did."

She laughed and wrapped her arms around me, giving me an enormous sisterly hug, telling me how very proud she was of me, that I had been so generous with a squirrel.

Heading onward, we caught up with the others. The older neighborhood kids had arrived at their destination tree only a few minutes earlier. One of the tallest boys grabbed the biggest monkey vine and climbed up the hill onto an embankment where he found an old root that made a perfect launching pad. Holding tightly onto the vine, and amidst the shouts of the other kids, he ran down the hill and launched himself way out, downward over the sloping hill to a small meadow-like open area in the forest below. At the farthest point, he let go of the vine and dropped gingerly to the ground, expertly landing as he had undoubtedly done many times before.

It looked like fun, but that vine was a little too high off the ground for me. And so, I entertained myself by swinging out on a lower monkey vine and practicing jumping off, which proved to be a blast. Karen followed, and we both had fun taking turns swinging on that vine.

We both also watched as Jackie patiently made her way to the front of the line for the highest monkey vine. She grabbed the vine, climbed the embankment, and quickly hurled herself into the forest. But she failed to let go and came flying backwards towards that big root. At that point, she let go, landing with an awkward thump and rolling sideways. Karen and I began running towards her, worried that she'd hurt herself. But she got up right away and we saw that she was okay.

Jackie immediately grabbed the rope and launched herself out for another try, this time letting go at the right time and making a perfectly soft landing. Before we could catch up to her, she ran and grabbed the vine again and made a third jump, once again letting go where all the kids did, dropping even more gracefully back to the earth.

The jumps had mussed up our hair and put dirt all over our knees, but of course, we didn't care. After I had swung and jumped my fill, I decided to climb a smaller tree with lots of branches not too far from where the others played. Ever timid, gentle Karen decided to follow me and together we simply watched the others.

Eventually, we kids got hungry and thirsty, and so, we headed for home. Karen stopped us after we got to the top of the concrete stairway and lovingly smoothed and straightened our hair and rubbed away all the dirt on our knees. Always gentle and loving, Karen hugged both Jackie and me. We trudged up the hill to our front yard and ended up pretty much looking like we'd simply been jumping rope and playing outdoors all day. Mother never knew that we had ventured off into the forbidden wild woods and that we had learned how to swing on a monkey vine and land safely on earth.

Chapter 5

THE QUESTION

When our new sister, Jenna, was born, even though I was just four years old, I knew that, since I was closest in age to the newcomer, the baby would be in large part "my" little sister. One cannot overstate the extreme excitement I felt about this! I loved my sisters deeply, and due to our family circumstances, trusted them more than anyone. At the age of four, I could hardly wait to become an "older" sister myself.

When Mother at long last carried baby Jenna into the house, I was prepared to love this baby with all my heart. How easy this turned out to be! Jenna was an unbelievably cute and adorable bundle of giggles and cuddles who would coo, smile, laugh, and delight the entire family. I became completely enthralled with her. I spent blissful hours amusing and engaging baby Jenna, gently marveling at her silky-soft skin and drinking in all the joy and love that in time we grew to share. When Jenna cried, I intuitively knew if she was hungry, in need of a diaper change, overheated, or simply fussing because she was overtired. It was typically I who alerted either six-year-old Jackie or our mother to attend to baby Jenna's needs that I couldn't handle.

Thus, a tight and loving bond grew between Jenna and me. It was this loving bond, and the obviously grave seriousness of Jenna's "high man" being broken, that made it paramount for me to find out exactly what that might mean. I began innocently posing the question to everyone and anyone who would listen:

"Hi. Do you know what a high man is?!?"

My mother tried to convince me that it wasn't my concern, that it truly didn't matter, that it was really nothing at all, and that Jenna was just fine. Good girls do not and must not ask that question of anyone. Of course, the odd tone in Mother's voice only served to intensify (not satisfy) my curiosity. Moreover, I wondered, *if it was really nothing at all, why had Mother been so upset that awful night?*

I first posed the question to my two best friends — my older sisters. Although they were very bright for their age, they also had no idea. And they also became curious. Jackie, the respected eldest and a sophisticate at the tender age of six, became curious enough to try a nonchalant approach. One day, while Mother was preparing dinner in the kitchen, Jackie acted in her most adult-like manner and tried to work it into the conversation in a most causal manner.

"Mother, what are you making?"

"I'm busy cooking. What do you need? I've made Spanish rice, one of your favorite dinners. Are you hungry?"

"Oh, yes, I am starved. I just love Spanish rice! What can I do to help?"

"Well, you can set the table. Dinner's almost all ready."

Jackie grabbed the plates and silverware and began setting the table. She walked back and forth from the kitchen to the dining room, carefully carrying plates, silverware, and glasses. She sauntered over to Mother, smiled, and said she was finished.

"What else can I do?"

"Well, you forgot the napkins, Jackie."

Jackie stood on her tiptoes to reach the napkins at the back of the counter and, carrying them in, finished setting the table. She walked back into the kitchen, sighed, and sat down at the kitchen table.

"Mother, I'm just curious. Not for any special reason. I was just wondering. Have you ever heard of a high man? What is it, a high man?"

Mother paused, put her paring knife down, and gave Jackie a long look. She called for her now-sober husband and gave him a long look, too, when he walked into the kitchen.

Mother spoke in a serious tone: "Jackie's asking what a high man is. Perhaps you'd like to tell her."

Father looked down at the girl from his tall stance and called me into the kitchen. In a grave tone, he announced that good girls don't ask such questions, and that they must never, EVER ask that question again, or else. It was one of those grownup things that children simply couldn't understand. If the questions persisted and the children were bad and didn't listen, they'd have to pay the price.

Jackie looked at both of them, cocked her head to one side, and made a decision.

"Okay," she said. "I won't ask again."

Jackie always was — and wanted to continue to be — a "good girl." Still, much to their deep dismay, my parents continued from time to time to hear my quiet, innocent inquiries of friends and other relatives. I was hopelessly curious, determined, and unstoppable.

At the next family gathering, which happened to be Christmas, I remained undeterred. Holiday preparations and celebrations were the best times in our house. Mother loved Christmas and allowed us three older girls to help trim the delicious pine Christmas tree. I particularly loved hanging the beautiful angel ornament who happened to have a halo and two open hands, holding a tiny, blank songbook. At least I imagined it was a songbook because I also loved the Christmas carols, so full of joy. Delicious pine fragrance filled me with happiness as I carefully hung her on the tree.

"Isn't she just beautiful, Karen?"

"Yes, I suppose she is. But you do know, angels aren't real." "What do you mean?" I asked. "They might be. You don't really know. There's a lot you don't really know yet."

"Well, believe what you want to believe," Karen said. "You'll understand when you're older."

Karen would sometimes gently remind me indirectly that the entire year between us made a world of difference in our understanding of most things. It remained, after all, an incredibly long timespan at that young age.

We had a whole Christmas Village that went under the tree. We had great fun placing the little houses, the church with its steeple, the manger, the tiny baby Jesus, and somber Joseph and Mary in just the right spots underneath the tree. We placed the Three Wise Men last and afterwards stood back and admired our miniature world underneath the tree. Mother also had a small ice-skating rink with skaters on it that we placed under the tree, and could play with, pretending that they were actually skating. A small sled and sled rider completed the village.

Although she allowed us to place the ornaments wherever we chose, Mother would singlehandedly finish the tree by placing shimmering, silver tinsel, one piece at a time, on the tree, to make it exactly as she wanted. A masterpiece, that tree filled our house with a delicious scent of pine and became a magical place for me. I could play and lose myself in the village underneath all by myself, moving the pieces about. I told made-up stories about the skater and the boy on the sled to baby Jenna who now could sit up and watch and listen. I kept her away from the pieces as she wanted to place them in her tiny mouth and chew on them. I had already learned a lot about little babies.

Christmas morning finally arrived. I had tried to stay awake to see Santa Claus but had failed. Still, as we ran into the living room, it became apparent that he had not failed us. I excitedly unwrapped fluffy pink slippers and a Slinky and the board game Chutes and Ladders and new pajamas and as always, my favorite gift — the delicious chocolates sent all the way from England by our Auntie Joan. She had been a lifelong pen pal of my mother's, and for some reason, every Christmas she sent a box containing a little lovely English gift for each of us girls, along with a generous amount of incredible English chocolates! This year, we older girls each received a beautiful, soft muff to keep our hands warm all winter long. Jackie's was aqua blue, Karen's a deep emerald, and mine a snowy white.

Soon the gifts had all been opened, including drawings that we had each made as Christmas cards for Mother and Father. After a hasty breakfast, I set about to seeing how many steps I could manage to make the Slinky crawl down. Karen came over and joined in my play, and eventually, Jackie picked up Jenna and came over, too. We took turns placing the Slinky at the top of the staircase and, of course, Jackie had the slinky coming down the greatest number of steps. We played with that amazing Slinky until Father complained about the noise:

"Let it rest for a little while, girls."

Later during that day, our Aunt Phyllis and Uncle John and their children, Eddie and Amy, stopped over with gifts for us. For me, Christmas that year had so far been fun and exciting. I always enjoyed seeing and playing with my cousins. Eddie, the oldest cousin in our entire extended family, walked through our door. With company there, I felt safe and emboldened, and I figured if anyone would know what a high man was, it might be Eddie. So, after the gifts were opened and the grown-ups were settled around the table drinking their coffee, I took Eddie over to the tree to give him a close-up view of the little village. Then, I quietly ventured to ask my question.

"Eddie, can I ask you a simple question?"

"Sure, you can ask me anything you want."

"What's a high man?"

I had been moving around the figures in the village under the tree, with my back to Eddie. He took me by the shoulders and turned me around.

"What did you say?" Eddie asked. "What is a high man?"

"Shhh, Eddie, please, what is a high man?"

Stepping back, he gave a little laugh, then proclaimed aloud that Susie was asking what a hymen was. I noticed Father coming towards us and Eddie, who was not answering my question, quietly told Father that I was asking what a high man was.

I grabbed my new Slinky tightly in my hand and bolted towards the steps, hoping to play with it and use it to hide in the staircase and escape any further attention. But Father, quick as always, grabbed my other hand and pulled me into the kitchen, closing the door behind us.

"I told you never to ask that question again!! Why can't you listen?"

He grabbed my other hand and squeezed it so hard that the Slinky nearly cut into my skin.

"Ouch! That hurts! Please don't!"

He lessened his grip and angrily took my Slinky from my hands. With no other witnesses, he bent it in such a way that it would never bring me (or my sisters) joy again. He hid it under the kitchen sink and turned back to frightened me.

"This is what happens to little girls who don't listen!"

And so, despite my best efforts, I learned nothing and lost my favorite Christmas toy.

But I did not, and could not cease to ask, even when harsh spankings and other punishments resulted. Time passed, and my curiosity remained unsatisfied. Thus, my quiet but urgent question would from time to time resurface.

"What IS a high man?"

Children in those days weren't the center of attention, nor were their words taken very seriously. Since a "high man" was exactly what my six-foot-two father was when he had consumed enough of his favorite beverage, beer, little attention was paid to my question at first. Yet, the question sometimes caused others to pause and wonder. Those who wondered did not respond nor act. Even so, as the months passed and I continued to ask, growing guilt and fear of discovery plagued Father.

One day, after several severe spankings and all other possible means of discouraging my questions were exhausted, Father began to feel truly desperate. He began joking about my demise and would make little gestures as if he were going to severely hurt me, such as waving a sharp knife a little too close to my face. He began to try to terrorize me into silence with his booming voice, his towering frame, and his threatening actions.

Summer finally arrived. Every year, our family drove up to "the Lake" to enjoy a vacation week with my father's parents, Grandma and Grandpa Ryan. They lived in a quaint retirement cottage that was walking distance from a good-sized lake. We girls simply adored our vacations at the lake! On the drive up, Father would always stop to pick up a gallon of delicious handmade, creamery ice cream. Although it was a long drive to get there, emerging from the car and smelling the country air made us girls all long to stay in the country forever!

We girls grew up as tomboys and wild as weeds. Unrestrained, we would dash into the two-story house (that my Grandpa had actually built) and head straight for the candy dish that Grandma always kept stocked with delicious sweets that, unlike anywhere else, we were allowed to simply help ourselves to. If it was a hot day, we'd hurriedly carry our small bags containing our swimsuits, pajamas, shorts and tops and, of course, hairbrushes and combs up the long staircase to the big open upstairs attic room. It had cots for us at the far end but mainly served as a storage area for our grandparents' off-season clothes and coats. The smell of mothballs assaulted my nose like a tidal wave, and I ran to the other end of the big room and threw open the window for relief. Fortunately, the moth balls were at the far end of this big second floor attic and wouldn't bother me when I slept (right under an open window). We'd change into our swimsuits and, dragging Mother along by the hand, head down to the lake as soon as we could!

These days in the country consisted of cool dips in the lake, running through the woods, eating fresh-picked food from Grandfather's garden, and letting our imaginations run wild. Sometimes, we'd fashion make-believe bows and arrows from sticks in the forest and pretend to be Indians, scouting about. Other times, we'd pretend to be wild horses, prancing through ancient woods. No matter our problems, we prided ourselves on being wild and free in that awesome forest!

On one such wonderful day, the whole family set out to take a long walk along the perimeter of the lake. Grandma and Grandpa decided to remain in the cottage with an eye towards relaxing. Besides, Grandma had already begun preparing a delicious dinner, complete with one of her mouthwatering homemade apple pies which sat on the countertop for all to admire.

To access the lake, we had to walk through the back yard, past the garden, across railroad tracks, and into the woods. On this particular walk, we found ourselves eventually hiking higher up than usual, at the edge of the cliff top overlooking the entire lake. At the summit, we all paused to admire the view. Mother cautioned everyone.

"Girls, don't go too near the edge!!"

All of a sudden, Father unexpectedly grabbed me by the shoulders, took me dangerously close to the edge and, to the horror of the others and with an evil smile on his face, made a loud joke about how easy it would be to accidentally bump me off the cliff. As he held me at the very edge, my mouth open but no scream escaping, I heard my terror-stricken mother and sisters screaming.

"Stop!" Mother begged. "It's not funny!"

For an agonizing moment, I could see in their eyes that they thought that he might actually do it. Finally, after thoroughly terrorizing everyone, he relented and let me go, laughing loudly to show that it had all been just an act, of course, all just a joke, a harmless joke. Thereafter, at times, he'd simply give me a rough shove in a wrong direction, towards a highway or a rushing stream and again evoke a scream from me and my sisters and Mother if they were present.

Unfortunately, I was not the sole witness to something that I didn't yet understand. I was just a Peetail, confused, and now also the scapegoat whenever Father felt the need for one for whatever was displeasing him in any particular moment, day or night.

Chapter 6
ALSO A HERO

I had a terrible time trying to learn to swim. The water in the lake was shallow at the edge so it was safe to swim and play in the shallow. My Grandmother, determined to teach me to swim, donned her old-fashioned swimming suit and ventured into the water with me.

"First you have to learn to float," she said. "Lie on your back."

She supported me underneath with her arms. In this way, I first floated. What a wonderful sensation, floating in the water. When she gently let her arms fall to her sides, I sank, quickly coming up, choking, and coughing up water. That day, she tried again and again to teach me to float on my own. But it was hopeless. To her great disappointment, I just couldn't do it.

Still, our parents allowed me to play and cool off in the lake with the others. My grandparents had a flat raft of sorts, and we were granted permission to use it. A few days after my floating failure, Karen and I borrowed the raft and, not paying attention, paddled out into the deeper water. Leaning over and looking at something in the water, I fell out of the raft and into the water. To my horror, the water was way over my head. I immediately began floundering.

My father, watching from the shore, jumped up and, taking giant leaps, raced into the water to rescue me. For me, on that awesome day, he became my hero. Being at his parents' house, Father, for once quite sober and not hungover, acted quickly in public to save one of his girls. Father respected his mother's wishes that he never imbibe while visiting with her at the lake. That was one of the most magical aspects of going to the lake!

Years later, I finally learned to swim while attending a YMCA camp for a week with my cousins. There, I received not only excellent instructions, but also had no choice. I had to dive into the water, as did the other teens. We had to follow precise instructions and stay afloat or suffer great humiliation and embarrassment. Needless to say, thanks to the YMCA, I finally learned to swim!

Chapter 7

AN UNINTENTIONAL DEATH

Easter always proved to be one of the best times of the year for us four girls. With the winter thawing, the weather warming, school about to end, and summer fun drawing closer, Easter marked the beginning of all things sunny and warm. On Easter morning, my sisters and I would awaken early and happily search for our own individual basket full of goodies left by the Easter Bunny.

Weeks ahead of time, Mother would sew a beautiful Easter outfit for each of us, and we would each get to buy new shoes, a matching hat, and purse. It was quite the affair! We loved going to church on Easter morning, feeling atypically proud in our crisp, new outfits on a fine spring morning. Sometimes, even on Easter, Father would sleep late and not go to church with us.

Easter afternoon included a delightful Easter egg hunt. Best of all, we girls loved the soft and cuddly live Easter ducks, which were bought every year only at Easter. We were each allowed to each pick out one duck, either a pink, blue, or yellow bird. Back then, the chicks were dyed pretty colors. We lovingly kept our baby ducks in a box. The ducks, though tiny, would grow quickly and shed their dyed fur, leaving a soft yellow coat. We girls cuddled them, played with them, and literally adored these special pets!

These Easter traditions were luxuries that, despite Father's expensive drinking habits, our parents somehow always managed to afford on his paint salesman's salary. Mother always tried very hard to keep up appearances, no matter what, and at certain important times, such as Easter, she succeeded.

We girls played with these ducks as one would play with a beloved toy and, being as maternal as we all were, we would make sure that our soft and fragile ducks were always lovingly returned to the safety of their box. There were three main rules: be gentle with one's duck; always put the duck back into the box; and clean up your duck's droppings.

We were also responsible for feeding and watering the ducks, which was also actually fun. Not so fun was the cleaning up of the duck droppings that resulted when the ducks were out of the box, but we three older girls tended to that faithfully, fearing

Father's harsh punishment if a mess was discovered.

In our joint bath at the end of one fine spring day, a place where we three older girls often also played, laughed and sang together, unattended and free, a song was born: "*Piddly doo doo doo doo, Piddly doo doo doo doo — every time I let out my duck, it piddly doo doo doos, piddly doo doo doos, every time I let out my chick, it piddly doo doo doos. . . .* " We were simply tired of cleaning up the duck dirt, and as we often did, made up a song about it, laughing and singing about it.

The gift of song, the gift of music, is one precious gift that we girls were given by both parents. Mother played piano and sang in a strong, high soprano voice, and Father sometimes joined in, singing with Mother and playing his harmonicas. He owned several.

He also enjoyed playing the clown and making others laugh. He would create such a good time and explored his music creatively. He played his harmonica in a band which unfortunately we girls never heard. The band made a record, which was rare in the 1950s. Mother was quite proud that the band had cut a record and told everyone about it. My parents talked about and had high hopes of "making it big" someday. He would play the harmonica, and Mother would play the piano and sing. Those musical interludes stood out as heavenly moments.

One year when we girls were a little older, Father sat all four of us down on the living room floor. He patiently taught each of us to play a different part, such as alto, soprano, tenor, etc., on the harmonica to a popular song of the day, *Little Brown Jug*. He orchestrated the harmonizing, and each of us practiced our part. It never quite made it to a recording, but we enjoyed playing one of his favorite songs with him, creating music together. I saw Father as an accomplished musician although, unfortunately, his record never made it big. Even so, music became one of the sweetest joys of my childhood.

One Easter, Mother cautioned me, time after time, NOT to handle my duck quite so often. I was very little, but stubborn and, at that age, I often did exactly the opposite of whatever I was told to do. I handled that duck as often as I pleased, and in fact, handled it even more due to Mother's reprimand. With four girls to manage, Mother left much of my care to my sister, Jackie, and she didn't see me picking up my duck much of the time.

That fateful day, in the middle of the kitchen, standing on the cold, hard, linoleum floor and amidst the confusing hubbub of activity around me, I was distracted for a moment and my beloved duck slipped from my hands. The tiny duck crashed onto the hard linoleum floor. I froze for the briefest moment and then scooped up my precious duck, nudging it gently, and hoping with all my heart that it would wiggle as it had. Holding it out to Mother who had come into the kitchen in response to my outcry, I looked up at her and asked the question I dreaded asking.

"Is she OKAY?"

Mother took my beloved duck from my hands and examined it. After a moment, she looked down at me and answered with harsh words more scathing than a slap.

"No, Susie, she is NOT OKAY!! You didn't listen to me, and now, her neck is broken. She's DEAD! I told you not to handle her so much. You didn't listen to me. And now, she's dead! You KILLED her!"

With a disgusted grunt, Mother turned on her heel and whirled around, leaving the room empty, save me for and my dead duck. Alone, I sat down on the floor in a state of horror, cradling the dead duck, and shock and guilt slowly enveloped me.

So, there it was! I was a murderer. I knew enough of the Ten Commandments even at that tender age to know that killing a beloved living creature was THE worst of all actions. I thought that, even though it was an accident, the duck's demise made me into a murderer. I had broken the commandment, "Thou Shalt Not Kill."

I now suspected that my parents had been right all along – maybe I was truly "bad." From that moment on, I believed that I was not only bad, I was also doomed to whatever befalls truly bad people, which I could only imagine and tried not to think about.

I had disobeyed as usual, and because of that disobedience, I alone had caused the death of my beloved duck, that delightful pet that I had loved with all my heart. The words *bad girl* engraved themselves upon my soul and seeds of self-disgust were sewn.

For the next few hours, I was in dread of the harsh punishment that would surely result. When none did, it only made matters worse. I knew then beyond the shadow of a doubt the depth of the evilness of my deed. Never before had I done anything so awful that it was *beyond* punishment.

And so I accepted that I was the bad one, the family scapegoat, the one everyone looked to first when any wrongdoing was committed. It would take four decades of living and years of therapy before I would realize that I had indeed been molded into – and not born as – the family scapegoat.

Chapter 8

THE TAPE

Despite everything, I remained simply unstoppable. I continued to ask the "what is a high man" question when I was ordered not to and the resulting spankings failed to lessen my need to know. I continued asking the question when I was put to bed without my teddy bear. I continued asking the question when I was slapped across the face for asking it. Nothing deterred me.

One night, just before dinner, frustrated and fearful over the continuing questions, Father violently grabbed me. Amidst Mother's protests and my sisters' screams, he snatched me up and shook me. He then grabbed a roll of wide masking tape and slammed me down onto a hard dining room chair. He took the tape and began taping it tightly over my mouth, adding several extra layers until it was thick and tight, and my mouth was completely and quite uncomfortably taped shut.

"There, that'll shut you up, at least for a little while!" he shouted. "Now you'll stop asking questions. Remove that tape before I say so and you'll get the beating of your life!"

Mother protested: "But she's only five years old. She won't be able to eat any dinner tonight!! She's too thin already. She has to eat!"

"Let her go to bed hungry tonight," Father growled. "Maybe that'll teach her to do what she's told and keep her mouth shut — unless she wants to starve to death!"

My sisters stood by helplessly, six-year-old Karen and seven-year-old Jackie. They were wide-eyed and scared but knew, as did I, that no one dared to remove that tape as long as Father was in his semi-drunken, angry state.

I sat alone on the couch in the living room that night as the rest of the family ate a tense, quiet dinner in the dining room. I was put to bed with that tape still tightly wrapped over my mouth, not able to brush my teeth or wash my face, and not knowing when, or even if, the tape would be removed.

I only knew that I dared not cry because now, I couldn't breathe through my mouth. With that tape tightly over my lips, I was forced to breathe through my nose, which was already habitually stuffy. If I cried at all and my nose became congested, I feared that I would suffocate. I couldn't cry, I couldn't eat, I couldn't drink and, of course, I couldn't talk.

Exhausted from the emotions of the day and from having no dinner or water, I climbed into my bed early that night. Although thirsty, hungry, and exhausted, I fell into a deep sleep.

In the middle of the night, when everyone else was sound asleep, I was roughly awakened by Father. It was dark but the moonlight coming through the window revealed his angry countenance. He carried me downstairs, where we were alone in a room lit only by a small nightlight. He set me down and towered over me.

"Are you pleased with yourself?" he demanded.

I shook my head no.

He smiled at that, seeing my fear, and looked deeply into my eyes, the sickening stench of the alcohol on his breath assaulting my nose.

"Do you still want to know what a high man is?" he asked quietly.

My innocent spirit still strong, I answered honestly and slowly gave him a nod.

Enraged, he grabbed me by the shoulders and shook me. Then, he quickly ripped the tape off my mouth, taking a layer of skin with it.

Next, his face bristling with razor-sharp whiskers, he roughly and lustily kissed me full-force on my now raw lips — a violently long, painfully deep, prolonged kiss that left my face reddened and painful, and my soul violated.

"Unless you stop asking questions," he threatened, "the next time the punishment will be much worse!"

Then, he let me go and shoved me out of the room, ordering, "Go back to your bed!"

I quickly ran off, crying now that I finally could and suffering from my aching mouth. I found my dolly in the dark in my room and clutched her to my heart, allowing her to linger there until the house became quiet.

Shaking and sobbing, I quietly left my bedroom and wandered through the dimly lit house, alone and afraid, gingerly touching my now freed but painfully raw face. Somehow, I found a glass, filled it with water and had a delicious drink. Then I used the toilet, splashed some cold water on my face, and made my way back to bed, where, with my stomach empty and my face afire, I quietly cried myself to sleep.

Father's violent reactions only increased my curiosity and served to strengthen my resolve. My mind had an unquenchable need to know. I knew from his actions — and from the cries of my baby sister and my mother's harsh words to him at the time — that it was something big and something important. Though my sisters begged me to please, please stop, I continued to pose the question of others whenever I could, albeit much more carefully and quietly.

At another family gathering, I asked my Aunt Annie, "What's a high man?"

Shocked, she repeated the question aloud, unaware of her loud tone. Mother and Father offered a quiet explanation, saying their daughter had no idea what she was saying, but after that, Father became increasingly rough with me.

On one drunken occasion, after he had his usual beer, he tried to set my hair on fire. He lit matches and had fun throwing them at my head, one after another, laughing as I dodged and the others screamed. On that occasion, there was no chance of escaping out a door, as had become my habit.

And so, eventually, my hair was indeed set on fire, amidst the chaos and terrified screams of Mother and my sisters who had been desperately trying to protect me. Mother stepped up and, using her bare hands, quickly put out the small fire, with no burns resulting, as only the tips of my long hair had been burned. I smelled it although I never really saw it. But I could also see the horror in her eyes and the eyes of my sisters.

"You've had your fun, Carl. Now, that's enough."

Much to everyone's relief, he stopped and had another beer, eventually passing out on the living room floor in his usual drunken stupor.

Another time, he yanked me sound asleep out of my bed so abruptly by one foot that I somehow didn't even awaken. He dragged me behind him down the steep, hard wooden steps, my head loudly banging on each step. I didn't wake up and was carried back up to bed when he was through terrorizing my mother, I suppose, by this — yet another demonstration of his absolute power.

Fear of discovery motivated my tormented father, and he knew that if he did not somehow stop those questions, confuse my mind, or somehow erase the memory of the incident, eventually his crime would mostly certainly be uncovered, his heinous act revealed, and possibly, repercussions could result.

One day, he devised a desperate plan to shut me up once and for all. Drunk and sweaty and reeking of beer, he carried out yet another heinous act of violence. The memory of that most heinous act, along with all the other equally violent ones listed above, would become lost, buried deeply in my mind — lost for more than thirty years, due to the brutality of his actions.

Their resurfacing is a most incredible tale of two turtles. Most importantly, their resurfacing meant that, in the final analysis, he had lost, and I had actually won! I had won because in the end, I HAD remembered everything and finally knew what a high man was and why it had been such an important secret.

Chapter 9

GOOD TIMES

During the course of their marriage, Mother had made a move to the country "to help Father's nerves get better." Father would often play hide-and-seek with us girls in the back yard, his lit cigarette sometimes revealing his hiding place as dusk was falling. It was he who built us a full-sized playhouse in the back yard, constructed with scrap lumber but big enough for us and a few friends to play in. It was complete with a door, windows, flooring and a little roof. It was a beautiful playhouse!

Once, when visiting our nearby cousins on my father's side, Father invited my sisters and me, all six of our cousins and several neighborhood kids into the back of a box-type van he was driving for work at the time. He told us to "relax" and enjoy the ride, although, with so many kids, it was standing room only. As the van moved slowly down the road, he zigzagged this way and that way, causing us to gleefully bump into and topple over onto each other, laughing and screaming. No one was hurt, and it was fabulous fun. Much to our disappointment, both our mother and our aunt forbade Father from ever doing THAT again. He took a tongue-lashing for his antics.

Nonetheless, it was such tremendous fun that we gave it a name. And thus, the "Relax Game" was born.

Thereafter, on any car trip where giggling was tolerated by our parents, we girls would sit on the edge of the back seat, closely together so that, at each turn, we could "relax" into each other, laughing and toppling, and having tremendously silly fun! These were, of course, in the days before seat belts were invented.

It was Father who would sometimes playfully hide and jump out unexpectedly and scare us girls, catching us unaware and laughing with us after our startled yelps had faded away. He also had a way of pulling down his one eye and eying a person up and down that never failed to make us giggle and laugh.

It was Father, not Mother, who sat us girls down, at a young age, and taught us how to play cards, Blackjack being his game of choice. We'd play for pennies which, in the end, were all returned to one pot to be kept for another day. Mother strongly disapproved of this, which, of course, made it all the more appealing to us girls and to Father.

"This is gambling!" she exclaimed loudly. "It's sacrilegious, and it's corrupting the girls' characters."

Father was not a dedicated churchgoer by nature, but the minister never gave up hope. He would occasionally drop by — unannounced — on Sunday to ask how we were all doing and to spread the Good Word.

One especially exciting Sunday afternoon, the church minister came a-knocking on our door during our Blackjack card game. Mother heard the knock, saw him through the window of the door and with a scared declaration, announced his arrival.

"Quick! Hide the cards!!!"

Father and we girls were well into the game, with cards and pennies spread out all over the kitchen table. With Mother's announcement, we all scrambled. Never did a table get so quickly cleared away!

The minister patiently waited at the front door, and Mother finally welcomed him into our house. She invited him into the kitchen to sit down, which he did.

"Would you like a cup of coffee?"

"Yes, please."

Coffee was served, and we girls listened from the living room. I thought it interesting that the minister sat and had his cup of coffee at the very table where, seconds earlier, nefarious gambling had taken place. As we eavesdropped on their conversation, we struggled to contain our giggles – unsuccessfully.

"What in the world might they be giggling about?" the minister asked.

Mother came in and yelled at us, then suggested we might want to go outside to play. And so, the minister never knew of the sinful game he'd interrupted nor fully understood the giggling coming from the living room.

Chapter 10

A CHILD WITHOUT
A BIRTHDAY

Baby Jenna's birthday was July 31ˢᵗ, and mine one week later, August 7ᵗʰ. Every year, for as long as I could remember, my mother never celebrated my birthday on my birthday. Every year, she combined my birthday celebration and Jenna's but always held them on Jenna's birthday, a week before my actual birthday.

At first, I didn't mind. I adored my little sister and making her wait a week to celebrate both birthdays on my day seemed somewhat selfish. Besides, Mother insisted that it was too much work to bake two cakes so close to each other. Initially, I had no objections since the cake bore both of our names and gifts did materialize for both of us.

But, after several years, I began wanting my "own" birthday and started asking for a party on MY birthday – just once. This may seem like a trivial thing to some. But try to imagine a childhood without ever – ever! – having a celebration or even recognition of one's own special birthday occurring on one's true birthday.

So, after several years of being an "add-on" to Jenna's birthday parties, I protested. I literally begged to have my birthday celebrated on *my* real birthday, August 7th, even just once!! But my mother always insisted on celebrating the two birthdays on my sister's day.

This left me with a deep sadness and a feeling that something was very wrong – with me. And so it happened that I felt I never really HAD a birthday as a child and most importantly, was never told the true reason why. In the absence of any meaningful explanation, I had no choice but to accept these circumstances. I could only wonder if perhaps I simply didn't deserve a birthday, considering all my bad actions.

It's silly, I know. Yet, the big July 31st celebrations *never* felt like my birthday celebrations. July 31st never felt like my birthday because it *wasn't* my real birthday. It was Jenna's. I was an add-on. On my "real" birthday, August 7th, no one would wish me a "Happy Birthday," not Mother, nor sisters, nor friends. No one empathized with my point of view.

I was told, "You already had your birthday."

This lack of my own special day affected me in such a profoundly deep way that I dream about it occasionally to this very day.

Turns out that, like most things in this life, it had absolutely nothing whatsoever to do with me. Sadly, for me, my mother didn't brave telling me the full truth until I was in my early forties. Finally, some honest truths emerged, and Mother at long last shared with my sisters and me the following painful events of her childhood.

On August 7, 1940, her adoring father, a grandfather whom I would never know, unexpectedly dropped dead from a heart attack while walking on one of the main downtown streets. My mother's world was irreparably shattered on that date.

His death had occurred several months after his elder daughter suffered a ruptured appendix. In 1940, penicillin was tragically not yet available to the general public. My mother's sister, Nora, had undergone surgery following the rupture of the appendix, but massive infection remained. While the family helplessly watched, Nora suffered an excruciating, eighteen-month ordeal of dying a slow death in her own bed at home.

The family desperately tried to help her. Every member of the family was horribly affected as they frantically tried to ease her agony. My grandfather blamed himself for the illness, because it was he who had given her a laxative when she had complained of abdominal pains. Unfortunately, soon after that, her appendix had ruptured and so, he was wracked with guilt and almost never left her side. He hardly slept or ate, ignoring his own health, and so he became so exhausted and run down that he died of a sudden heart attack on August 7, 1940.

This occurred many months before Nora would follow him into death from an illness that penicillin, available at that time only to World War II servicemen, could have cured. At the time, my mother was the tender age of thirteen. Her father's death hit her doubly hard, because she had been "Daddy's Girl," and she had adored him. After he passed, my mother and her mother and brothers were overwhelmed with not only the grief of his passing but with continuing to care for the slowly dying Nora. And so it was that my mother was — long before any of us were born and unbeknownst to me until I was in my forties — emotionally mutilated from these events.

After her father's death followed months later by the death of her sister, Mother had been forced to wear black and only black for a painfully long period of time. That experience inspired a vow to never ever wear black again! She owned not one item of black clothing! She loathed it and the grief that it represented that much.

My birth occurred thirteen years to the day after a grandfather I would never know had unexpectedly died at a time when his family had needed him the most. Never really recovering from her father's death, Mother couldn't bring herself to celebrate a birthday or anything else on August 7th. And that was why I would never have my own childhood birthday and moreover, would never even know the true reason for such for several decades. I had assumed that it must have been related to something that I had done. It left an emotional hole in me, passed onto me by the emotional hole in my mother. It also left unanswered questions and deep confusion. I guess the greater part of me felt that I simply didn't deserve my own special birthday.

This story is a strange one, but it also makes one wonder about the human mind, about love, and most importantly, about the unseen hands. The most amazing part of this story is actually not yet told. It involves a new-found friend, a gypsy woman at the beach, a painted turtle, and the last piece of the unsolved puzzle. As a child, I never discovered the answer to my "high man" question. In fact, evil deeds caused that most pressing question to become buried in my mind, forgotten and lost for decades.

Chapter 11

A COURAGEOUS MAN

Mother began working outside of the home when Jenna was old enough to be left with a neighbor. Jenna always considered herself one of the very first "latchkey" children and deeply resented it.

When I turned eleven years old, many years after Mother began working outside of our home and years after she had begun counseling, Mother at long last mustered enough courage to take her four girls and leave our violent father. We fled and sheltered for weeks with one of my aunts and uncles and their six children until Mother saved up enough money to rent a place. We then moved into a small apartment where, from time to time, Father showed up at the door dead drunk, necessitating a call to the police. I was terrified that he would gain access and beat Mother and us.

One day, Mother brought home a big box of food, relieved that she had received her first FREE box of groceries from The Salvation Army. We girls happily joined in, unpacking the box and checking out the cereal and other items. We saw a jar of peanut butter and eagerly opened it and spread it onto white bread. My joy quickly turned to horror, as I realized that I simply could not swallow that extremely dry and tasteless peanut butter.

"This is awful!!" I exclaimed. "This is the worst peanut butter I have ever tried to eat. It sticks to your mouth and tastes like paste. I'll starve to death before it eat it!!"

Mother's face fell.

"Don't be so picky!" Karen snapped. "I don't think it's that bad at all." She even managed to eat it with a grin, smiling at Mother and pretending it was delicious.

Minutes later, she herded me into the bedroom to explain.

"Look, I'm really sorry that I yelled at you, but the truth of the matter is that we do not have enough money for food. We're darn lucky that we're getting the free food, even if it's not the best. Did you see how sad Mother looked when you said that you would not eat it?"

I hung my head and nodded. As usual, Karen was right, and I stopped complaining. By the way, I did not eat any of that peanut butter. I tried, but it was just too dry, and I could not get it down.

Somehow, we persevered, albeit on free food from The Salvation Army and hand-me-downs from friends and family. Most weeks, our sustenance mainly consisted of that box of food from The Salvation Army. As my older sisters forced down that peanut butter, washing it down with the watered-down powdered milk, we all dreamt of better days. We knew that at the moment, poverty engulfed us, despite Mother's hard-working efforts and steady salary. We worried as we barely scraped by.

The months passed, and we five continued to survive in our little apartment, consuming the free food, and thankful that Mother didn't succumb to Father's periodic pleas to return to him. I held my breath every time he stood at the front door, begging her to reconsider. Extreme relief washed over me as I heard that door at long last slam.

In addition to trips to The Salvation Army, we also went to the Brookline United Presbyterian Church on Sundays where I prayed for safety and better days. I liked that church and felt comfortable and safe there. Some of my schoolmates also attended so I felt a sense of belonging there.

One Sunday, I was standing in the vestibule after the service when a fellow approached Mother.

"Hi, Lisa. Do you remember me?"

"Oh, sure. Hi, Greg. How are you doing?"

"I'm doing swell. I'm an Elder here at the church. Hey, are these girls all yours?"

"Yes, they are," she said with a sigh.

"Well, you have a fine family, Lisa."

"Thanks, Greg. See you later. Let's go, girls."

As she ushered us all out, I curiously asked, "Who was that handsome man, Mother?"

"Oh, he was the class clown in high school – a real goof. Don't mind him."

She was neither impressed nor interested. That old high school acquaintance, a tall fellow named Mr. Greg Smith, had indeed been the class clown during their high school years. We later learned he had left high school during his senior year to help defeat the Nazis during World War II. To me, Greg was a strikingly handsome man with a strong chin and chiseled features. He had a deep and caring voice. I liked him a lot.

He approached us on many other occasions at church. We began sitting with him in the pew. He also came over to our apartment a few times and sat with Mother on our shabby couch, talking long after we girls had gone to bed. We all liked him, and although I felt extremely shy around him, it was evident that he — a good man — also cared for my mother.

The next thing I knew, he and Mother - to my immense joy — announced that they were getting married!

As an Elder in the church, Greg often and most impressively read scripture in front of the congregation. Sober and hard-working, he proved himself over time an honest, strong, and fearless man. He borrowed enough money from a friend to make a down payment on a big duplex house, and we all moved into the upstairs apartment, beginning a better life and feeling a delicious relief that The Salvation Army peanut butter had become a thing of the past!

One day soon after we had settled into our new lives, the doorbell rang, and my new dad Greg went down the steps to answer the door. I peeked around the corner of the L-shaped staircase and watched.

"Hi, Carl, how are you doing?" Greg quickly suspected that my father had been drinking.

"I'm okay," Father said. "Just thought I'd stop by and see my girls."

"I'm sorry, Carl. You can't come in here when you're drunk."

"Awww, come on. Just for a minute. I just want to see them for a minute."

Father hung his head in shame.

"Carl, the rule is – you can't see the girls if you've been drinking. That's the way it's going to be. Sober up and come back and then you can see them."

To my amazement, my father, who had broken down doors and pushed his way through doors, who had bullied and hurt me and my sisters and my mother, simply turned around and left!

Hooray!

My new dad – many inches shorter than my father – had fearlessly stood up to him! And this would only be the first of many such occasions.

My dad Greg had shown no fear. I had seen that he was a kind, patient, and hard-working man. Now I knew that he was also a courageous one, a proud Veteran of World War II. He had impressed me from the very first time we had all encountered him in church and now, as our protector, he became my hero.

And so, my dad Greg never ever allowed my father to come into our home or in any way come into contact with my sisters and me unless he was stone cold sober. Greg provided Mother and us with a fine and secure home, and for the first time, I actually felt safe at home.

Chapter 12

ADOPTION

Eventually, Greg decided he wanted to adopt the four of us, but only if we all unanimously wanted to be adopted. Jenna very much did, and my two older sisters expressed willingness. However, I felt that I couldn't turn my back on our birth father. I loved and respected Greg but, despite everything, I also loved my birth father. My sisters argued with me to change my mind and were angry with me. But I felt deeply sorry for our drunken father who had literally lost everything, including his own self-respect. Despite all the hurts of the past, part of me loved him and knew that part of him loved us and so, I fearfully declined the adoption.

Greg's response? He showed me compassion and understanding. He even stood up for me against my outraged sisters.

"Hey!!!" he said. "If she doesn't want to get adopted, that's okay. She might change her mind. I'll adopt all four of you, or none. Everyone has to be comfortable with it before we can proceed. That's just the way it is."

And so, that stood – and my sisters were no longer angry with me (not that they expressed anyway).

His loving response and patience, in time, changed my mind. A year passed and when the subject arose once again, this time I agreed to the adoption.

What an amazing day that was – watching each of my older sisters swearing to tell the truth and taking the stand and testifying. And then, my turn arrived. Being sworn in inside a solemn courtroom and testifying in front of everyone that yes, I did indeed choose to be adopted by my stepfather, Greg Smith, remains something that I'll never forget.

Afterwards, we enjoyed a rare splurge. He took the entire family out to dinner at an expensive restaurant, and we all celebrated the adoption. In those days, dining out was a luxury, not a weekly or even monthly occurrence, but one saved for very special occasions.

I made the right choice, and in time, I came to think of Greg as my "real" father and the other as my (unfortunate) "birth" father. What a blessing he proved to be to my mother and to us four girls who had been barely surviving on Salvation Army peanut butter and nights filled with terror when we would hear our drunken father yelling, threatening us from outside our door.

Chapter 13

COLLEGE

Decades passed, and young womanhood descended upon us four girls. Jackie wed at age eighteen and left home. Karen went to college and decided to live on campus. However, she did not attend classes as expected but ended up wasting our parents' hard-earned tuition money for that first full semester that she lived — and partied — on campus. Unfortunately, my parents didn't discover the fact that she wasn't attending classes until it was too late to obtain a refund for that semester. Thus, Karen wasted a great sum of their money and even worse, shook their faith in their daughters' commitments to their respective educations.

Due to Karen's unfortunate wasting of those initial college funds that my parents had paid, they didn't even discuss college with me during my senior year. It appeared to me that they had indeed decided that a college opportunity would not be offered to me. And so it was that eventually, I got a job and found myself still living at home long after all my other sisters had left.

I became very depressed and found myself eating too much and gaining weight. One day, I felt so disgusted with myself that I flung a rope over a basement rafter, put the rope around my neck, and jumped! After the rope broke due to my enormous and disgusting weight, I burst into tears, despairing that I couldn't even do THAT right! I went through a long period of depression.

Eventually, Mother talked me into joining a gym with her, and I began exercising and snapping out of it. The endorphins kicked in, and the weight began to come off. I stuck with that gym routine and gratefully recovered.

A few months later, I read an article about depression, and adding onto suggestions listed in that article, I compiled a list of daily steps that anyone can take to help PREVENT depression. I also determined that if I ever felt myself becoming depressed again at any point in life, I would follow these seven steps religiously. They are:

1. Get plenty of rest;

2. Drink lots of water;

3. Get some exercise every day (stimulate endorphins);

4. Do something fun (or at least enjoyable) every day;

5. Spend some quiet time alone each day;

6. Do something sociable every day (example: call a friend); and

7. Eat smaller quantities of food but more often (five to six times a day).

Life went on and a beloved wealthy uncle decided to finance a year of college for me to see if that might help me find a path. He did this with the understanding that my parents would then pick up the cost of the subsequent years. He had attended Penn State University and with my uncle's encouragement, I applied there and was accepted. It proved to be an interesting and life-changing experience, living in a dormitory and attending classes, making friends, and being back in school again.

At the end of my first year of taking liberal arts classes, however, I still had no idea of what I wanted to do with my life. I felt that I could not, in good conscience, allow my parents to spend their hard-earned money on me when I didn't have a clear-cut goal in mind. And so, I dropped out of college, returned home and found another job.

Eventually, I left home, got married, and had two wonderful sons who are two years apart. My husband worked for his father, constructing houses, and had an unfortunate accident in 1976. Three men were down in the hole, awaiting the steel beam that would be lowered into it, steadied by them, and then set in place. My husband was on the upper end, directing the crane operator and steadying the heavy beam.

Unfortunately, the beam, once placed, slipped on soft ground and he, a strong fellow, grabbed for it and steadied it out of fear that the men in the hole would be crushed. Almost immediately, he began having back pain, but it took more than a year for doctors to reach a "ruptured disc" diagnosis. By then, severe nerve damage had occurred.

This traumatic experience reminded me of my mother's saying about people. If a friend was stingy and so were the parents, then, the friend "came by it honestly," and one had to forgive and overlook the stinginess since it was "come by honestly."

As to my husband, he came by the ensuing drug dependency honestly, as the result of a heroic act. His pain was tremendous and back then, medicine couldn't adequately help him. He could no longer work, so I took a job at a law firm, and he stayed at home with our sons, unable to handle even the cleaning or the shopping because of his pain. Eventually, unbeknownst to me, prescription drugs turned into illegal drugs.

At one point, we moved out into the country, hoping the peace and quiet would reduce his pain. There, the burning of garbage was permitted. One chilly night, I grabbed his black spring coat, went out to burn the garbage, and headed up the hill. I put my hand in the pocket and pulled out a black vial that contained a white substance. I couldn't be sure, but I suspected it was cocaine. When I asked him, he admitted that he had indeed been procuring and ingesting cocaine for his pain.

As I had been working for a law firm, supporting the family for many years after his accident, I'd learned a thing or two about the law.

"We could lose the boys," I warned, "if the cocaine is found in your possession and we are both arrested."

Aghast that his prescription drugs had turned into illegal drugs, I gave him an ultimatum: "Give up the cocaine or I will be forced to leave."

A week later, I discovered more cocaine in the house and my decision about my future was made for me.

My husband had a cocaine problem that he refused to acknowledge, and I had two sons to raise. I bravely took my two young sons and on only a legal assistant's salary, set out on my own to support both them and me.

My husband received worker's compensation for his injury but refused to pay any child support. It took many years of petitioning in court to obtain any funds and once again, I found myself living on not Salvation Army peanut butter this time, but peanut butter (and other food items) that I gratefully attained from the local food bank for many years.

Chapter 14

MEMORIES REEMERGE

The reemergence of shocking, long-buried memories resulted quite simply through love, made possible by loving thoughts, experiences, decisions, and finally, loving, selfless acts.

The first to reemerge concerned not me but my older sister, Jackie. At that time in my mid-thirties and eighteen months divorced, I found myself falling deeply in love with a good, decent, hard-working, and fun-loving man who would eventually become my second husband. We talked and laughed, spending long and wonderful hours together. We had much in common, including that we had both conquered one of the strongest addictions — nicotine addiction. Back then, one rarely encountered an ex-smoker, and this doubtless increased our mutual respect. Our relationship deepened and became one full of trust and affection.

One day, after a particularly fun afternoon spent together, an odd and inexplicable realization dawned on me. I'd been discussing with Tomas the fact that I felt profound gratitude that, more than a decade ago — and only after at least five or more serious attempts at quitting smoking — had I been able to actually overcome the cigarette habit. Even after quitting, one must continue to fight the urge, for weeks and months – no easy task!!

In 1976, two months after I'd quit during the course of my first marriage, I'd been blessed with my first pregnancy, and I found myself with the absolute best incentive to continue to avoid cigarettes!!! Eventually, I felt confident that I had TRULY won out over the addiction. I found myself extremely grateful, since at that time, the dangers of second-hand smoke had become known and I had had a wonderful, healthy new baby to love and nurture!

Tomas listened thoughtfully, as he always did, asking questions about how I'd managed to quit. He also shared his long-past experiences with quitting smoking. As my dear Tomas and I were snuggling and watching TV, he brought up how difficult it had been for him to quit the cigarette habit. He had accomplished it cold turkey, the first time he'd tried.

I was repelled even hearing the words "cigarette habit" coming out of his mouth. My heart began to pound. I suddenly became aware that part of me was in a deep sense actually feeling *afraid* of cigarettes. This fear of cigarettes was inexplicable!

What an odd thing! I thought. *Why should I be AFRAID of cigarettes? I conquered that habit a long time ago.*

This fear deeply troubled me because the feeling persisted but, at the same time, made absolutely no sense. Why would anyone be deeply *afraid* of cigarettes — especially me, someone who had successfully overcome the nicotine habit?

As an adult woman, when I snuggled at long last safely in the arms of a man who loved me, protected me, and who would one day become my cherished second husband, I remembered that I was *afraid* of cigarettes. Then, with a jolt, sometime later, I remembered why!! I remembered seeing our father burn my sister, Jackie, with his cigarette! Odd that I didn't recall it until I was beyond thirty years old. These traumatic memories, including the morning he tortured Jackie with a cigarette burn as he lounged in the hammock, remained suppressed for decades, and shocked me severely when they reemerged.

In the 1950s, most kids loved playing outside and got out every chance they had. And most parents were extremely happy to get the kids "out of their hair" and so, we ran free and unsupervised. In our own backyard, we girls also enjoyed a swing set that sat off to one side near the property line. We could swing and go down the slide as often as we wanted, provided our beds were made and our chores had been done. Outside, we felt safer because we were in a better position to run and get away from our father, if need be.

My sisters and I would play outside every chance we could get, also because we felt a bit safer outside where one could run if need be. One sunny, summer day, my sister, Jackie, and I were playing quietly outside, swinging on the swings. Father lounged in his hammock on the back patio, once again severely hung over because of his beer. He was in a mean mood. We'd often manage to play quietly when he was hung over because we had witnessed his cruelty and knew that, although he could be loving and affectionate, he could also be irritable and fearsome and violent.

He lounged in that hammock lazily, unshaven and reeking of alcohol. Half asleep, he began watching us as we swung on our swings and slid down the slide, having fun. But the fun was not to last.

"Jackie, come here!" he said.

Jackie abruptly jumped off the swing and went cautiously over to our father.

"Yes, Daddy?"

"Be an angel and go inside. Fetch an iced tea for me, will you?"

"Sure, Daddy!"

Inside she went, to fetch an iced tea from Mother. It looked as if Mother had filled the glass a little too full as Jackie walked slowly and carefully out the side door and through the yard to the back patio. I slowed down my swinging and, from my perch on the swing, watched her. Jackie with her long, curly hair and beautiful smile, proudly delivered it without spilling a drop, which seemed an almost impossible task to me as I sat, still swinging and observing.

She handed him the glass and then, an odd thing happened. He took a long drink, set the glass down, and pulled Jackie closer to him. The stench of alcohol and his roughness caused her to push away from him, to try to get away. But he was forcing my sweet sister to linger, pulling her closer to him and rubbing his razor-like whiskers on her tender face.

"Ouch! Your whiskers are hurting me!"

She was trying to push away from him so that she could run. The iced tea now rested on the small table, and next to it, his ashtray contained a lit cigarette. With his free arm, Father picked up the lit cigarette and took a drag from it, inhaling deeply, still grasping her with the other arm. As he exhaled and she struggled, he became angry.

"How dare you resist me?!"

With a hideous smile on his face, he grabbed Jackie even more tightly and my beautiful sister Jackie screamed in agony as he intentionally pushed his cigarette into her upper arm! Mother came running out.

"What happened?"

"Jackie backed into my cigarette!"

"Oh, Carl — you should be more careful!"

"It was an accident, Lisa. She backed into it. It happened so fast. It's not my fault."

"You have to be more careful with your cigarettes, Carl!"

As she angrily escorted a whimpering Jackie inside, my sister said, "He burned me on purpose."

"Nonsense," our mother replied, and proceeded to chastise Jackie for being so careless as to brush into his lit cigarette. Not only had Jackie suffered a horrible burn, she was now being blamed for it and yelled at. Mother chose to believe, or at least pretended to believe, that it had been an accident. She took Jackie inside to tend to the excruciating wound. That first burn would heal, but the psychological and physical scarring it caused never really would. That ran way too deep.

Many years later, only after we were adults and I began writing, did I realize just how deeply she had been injured. I asked her for her good memories of our childhood to include them in my writing.

"I have absolutely no positive memories whatsoever from our childhood," she replied.

Even after I reminded her of some of the good times, she could not recall what I described. I suppose that she always had an eye and ear on our predatory father, forever fearful of his unpredictable behavior. Although she had somehow made me feel somewhat safe at times, if nothing else but by being the center of attention and thus the object of his focus, no one had performed that function for her. No one protected her and she never felt safe. It affected her every waking minute then – and continues to do so today – as the subconscious controls us in ways that we all remain unaware of. A lack of safety in childhood is a scar that, like the cigarette burn scar, never completely goes away.

That day, after Mother took Jackie inside, I remained unprotected outside in the sunshine, no longer swinging and enjoying the warmth of the day. I simply sat on the swing, transfixed, desperately hoping that by not moving, I could somehow make myself invisible. But unfortunately, he had noticed that I had seen. I couldn't ingest the horror and cruelty of what I alone had just witnessed and hoped that by not moving I might somehow escape his hideous attention.

After eyeing me for a long moment, he rose and took a drink of iced tea and began walking towards the swing set. He picked me up off the swing. He roughly carried me to a more secluded corner of the back yard, his towering six-foot frame seeming larger than ever. The depth of the terror I felt in that instant surpasses the power of description. I thought he would burn me, too.

To my immense relief, as he put me down, he also lowered the hand that still held the lit cigarette.

Towering over me, he spoke in a deeply deadly serious tone.

"If you ever (pause) EVER tell ANYONE what you just saw — (pause) I will kill you!"

"Do you understand? I WILL kill you!"

I couldn't speak, so I nodded. Even in my shocked state, I definitely understood. I knew beyond the shadow of a doubt that he would kill me — he surely would — and that no one would be able to stop him. I had been watching as he had deliberately pushed his lit cigarette into Jackie's arm, severely burning her and causing her to scream in agony. I alone had witnessed it.

He turned and returned to the hammock, and I got out of that back yard as quickly as I could, running into the house, wanting to run and tell Mother the truth, but knowing that I could not. I ran into the bathroom and shut the door, at long last feeling some semblance of safety.

I gazed into the mirror and saw the shock that had been inflicted on me. My eyes held both terror and a deep sorrow, and I debated with myself silently about what I should do next. The little girl with the green eyes looking back at me looked beyond terrified. I tried to tell her that she needed to tell the truth about what she had seen, that Jackie had spoken the truth, and that none of us was safe. My mother needed to know it.

I watched my tears as they fell. Unable to stop them, I hid in our home's only bathroom until I heard a knock on the door and a soft voice asking to use the bathroom. That jolted me away from the mirror and my agonizing debate. I splashed some water on my face, washing away the tears, blew my nose, flushed the toilet, and opened the door.

I didn't tell my mother and in fact, told no one. Oddly, the memories of that horrid day eventually became buried deep within my innocent mind and became forgotten, literally for decades.

When I remembered them, my first reaction was to share these horrific memories with Jackie, who expressed oceans of relief and gratitude that someone else finally knew the truth. At long last, she felt validated. When I shared these memories with my two other sisters, my mother, and other family members, serious shock waves reverberated throughout the entire extended family.

One uncle's reaction was to implore me, "For God's sake, please never write about any of this."

Mother's reaction was that she didn't remember anything at all. Jackie who, of course, had never forgotten those burns, not to mention the other horrors, remained deeply grateful that someone else finally spoke the truth out loud.

"You must be becoming healthier," she said lovingly, "both mentally and emotionally. Your recollections, though upsetting, are indeed a massive step towards improving emotional health."

Chapter 15

MORE MEMORIES REEMERGE

It was long known that my two older sisters had been abused by Father — sexually abused. My oldest sister, Jackie, had been poked and forced to touch certain private parts and my second older sister, Karen, had been poked, through her clothing, in certain private parts. Father would come home drunk late at night, fall into bed with one or the other of the two oldest girls and violate them in this way or that. Mother was supposedly asleep.

Both sisters only spoke of this after they had become adults and, although what they spoke about didn't seem too terribly horrible to me, it was accepted as truth. It was general knowledge that they had each been "molested" by our father, but that my younger sister and I had not.

I married a wonderful man, Tomas, who made me feel safe enough that traumatic memories surfaced. Tomas made me feel secure enough that I eventually had the confidence to save up lots of money, quit my full-time job, and return to college. Working part-time and going to school part-time, I completed a bachelor's degree that I had been working on from time to time throughout my adult life.

I enrolled at Penn State University for the fall of 2001 and enjoyed part-time work and part-time classes until I finished my degree. Classes began just a few short days before 9/11! In fact, I was driving to school that first week when I heard the unbelievable news over the radio that airplanes had crashed into the World Trade Towers. Had I known how the world would change after those horrific events, I wonder if I would've risked quitting my full-time job to complete my degree and begin a new career.

In one class, there was another adult student, June, who was pregnant. She and I, being older than the other students, chatted and became acquainted. Early in the semester, she took a vacation to Atlantic City with her husband, and I offered to tape the class so that June wouldn't miss any vital information. Students often taped the lectures in addition to taking notes, as a type of back-up, so this wasn't at all unusual. June greatly appreciated my offer and while she was absent, I proceeded to record the lectures.

When June returned from vacation, she had a gift to give to me from a stranger she had met at the beach, along with the oddest story to share.

June had been walking on the boardwalk on the beach on a brilliant, sunny day. To her amazement, as she passed by a seated old woman, the stranger stopped her and asked her if she knew someone named Susie who was having problems.

June responded, "Yes!" and stopped to talk with this stranger, who from a distance would eventually change my entire outlook on my life.

What follows is my day-to-day (or more so, week-to-week) diary of that amazing change, and my actual personal diary that began in 1975 when I was twenty-two years old.

CHRONICLING MY JOURNEY TO REMEMBERING
Diary Entries

Dear Reader:
  Please keep in mind that this deeply personal diary was never intended to be published.

ed.

August of 1975: I have met a very interesting fellow. Peter is a carpenter who works for his father's company. Today, he doesn't make much money, working with and helping to supervise the crews that build new, luxury houses for his dad's business, but someday, when the business is his, he will make just as much money as his dad does now. Yet, at the present time, he actually makes much less money than the other workers employed by his father.

I must admit, I'm not so crazy about Peter's family. They're sort of a colder type of people, but

Peter is one of the hardest working men I have ever encountered. What really impressed me the most is how he takes care of his little brother, Kyle, and his little sister, Melissa, just like I had deeply cared for my little sister, Jenna.

Their mother died about a year ago in a car crash on her sister's birthday. The two had been out "celebrating" the birthday, drinking. The mother was driving and lost control of the automobile while negotiating a curve. Her sister survived the crash but Peter's mother, Janis, did not. The entire family was devastated by the loss, and after a year, they are still devastated.

The hardest thing Peter ever had to do in his entire life, he told me, occurred soon after his mom's death. He hopes he never has to do anything similar ever again. He walked into a room, looked into eight-year-old Kyle's eyes and seven-year-old Melissa's eyes, and told them that their mother was dead. Their ensuing sobs tore his heart into shreds, the pain of which is still quite evident.

Apparently, his parents' marriage had been on again, off again. They had separated and then reconciled many times over the course of years. They were in one of their separation phases when Peter's mom had died. His father had refused to pay for the funeral. Peter was determined to give her a decent funeral and paid for it himself. He's the oldest of five children, consisting of four older boys and then, little Melissa.

Thereafter, Peter acted more like a parent than a brother to Kyle and Melissa. For this, and many other reasons, I find I am falling in love with him. His two little siblings melt my heart. They are both very affectionate, and I have already begun to cuddle and nurture those two adorable motherless children. If I ever have a little boy, I told Kyle, I hope that he will be just like him. Melissa's a bit spoiled but cuter than cute, nonetheless. She has this thing, where she loves to unroll (and waste) toilet paper. I can't figure that one out.

April of 1981: Peter and I have been living in the downstairs apartment of my parents' duplex since he can't work and disability doesn't pay much. Unfortunately, while on antibiotics for a UTI, my IUD birth control failed, and I became pregnant – the last thing that we need!!

When I went to the Free Clinic for medical care, they told me that often, getting pregnant with an IUD results in a miscarriage and that that can occur when the IUD is pulled out. I held my breath when that doctor pulled that IUD out, but no miscarriage occurred. He actually advised me to have an abortion, but in my mind, that would be murder and although I respected others' rights to make their own decisions, it wasn't for me. I didn't want to live with that.

When we learned that it was twins, we really became concerned but still hoped for the best. I began bleeding at five months and had to be hospitalized. After a month in the hospital on medication that was intended to stop the contractions I'd been having, I lost the babies on April 18th – two boys! They gave us the choice to see them or not. Peter declined, but I wanted to see them.

They didn't look quite human at all! They looked more like odd little creatures to me. They had a torso, but only these little, tiny beginnings of arms and legs. It made me realize that women who have abortions are not murderers because these weren't yet humans, even after five months.

Being in the hospital for a month was such an ordeal. I've been so depressed because I love being a mother and having babies. The only bright spot is my little Lee who, at two and a half, is still enough of a "baby" that I can cuddle and snuggle and baby him. Also, Peter has been unusually kind lately, even buying me clothes that we really can't afford, which has cheered me up a bit. I long for a baby and wish I hadn't lost the twins.

※

March 1, 1985 (four years later): With great regret, I am taking our two sons, Jack and Lee, and leaving Peter. I hung in there for eight years after his failed back surgery. I am not sorry that I did so. It was the right thing to do, living the "for worse" part of those "for better or for worse" marriage vows. For eight years, I have supported him and the boys. In addition, I did all of cleaning, cooking, laundry and all of the housework. I had to.

Peter is in constant pain and has used pain medication regularly for several years. Unfortunately, the medicines no longer help him much, and he is very verbal in front of the boys about the degree of the pain he endures.

Recently, I discovered a vial of cocaine in a pocket of his coat. I let him know that I could not and would not chance going to jail on a drug charge, thus possibly losing my sons. When I asked him, "Who will raise our sons if we are both in jail?" he promised me that it would never happen again. He looked me in the eye and promised that he would stop using the cocaine.

A week later, when I again found cocaine in the house, I tried to get him to go to Narcotics Anonymous. He not only refused to go but physically barred my way and prevented me from going to a support group for those who love those who are addicted. That made my decision for me. I am thus marching forth on March 1st and leaving him. I am scared to death at the thought of trying to make it alone on my own with sole responsibility for the boys.

July of 1985: Unfortunately, Peter never rallied. In trudging through the divorce, I took the boys to Families in Transition, an excellent family counseling center geared towards making certain that children of divorce do not blame themselves for the divorce of their parents. Interestingly, we were shown a movie that reminded me of my childhood. It was exactly on point. So much so that I took my mother and three sisters to see it. Afterward, we were sitting out front at Mother's house, discussing the movie, when my Mother dropped a bombshell.

In our third decade of this life, we girls now learn that our sister, Karen, is not our full sister. She is our half-sister. The weird thing is that Mother told the whole story as if she was actually proud of it. You should have seen my adopted dad's, her husband's, facial reaction to the news. I fear he lost much respect for my mother on this day. She told us facts that, some might contend, she should have taken to her grave, forever unspoken.

She and my birth father, Carl, had tried and tried to have children. She had suffered miscarriage after miscarriage. At that time, they were good friends with a minister and his wife, Oliver and Florence. (She later revealed that Oliver had had the same disease as my birth father, alcoholism.) She and my father were very involved in Oliver's church, with the youth group and other activities.

I can't say if it was or wasn't the result of prayer, but apparently my mother became pregnant by my birth father, Carl, with my sister, Jackie, and perhaps with the extra support of good friends, successfully gave birth to her first baby.

Oliver and Florence were in due time also blessed with a baby, a son, Oliver, Jr. Florence experienced psychological and emotional problems after the birth which prevented her from being an affectionate mother. Mother had volunteered to and slipped seamlessly into an affectionate maternal role with baby Oliver, filling that gap left by Florence's emotional problems.

In together caring for and nurturing this new baby and because Oliver was such an excellent father, my mother claimed, she fell deeply in love with the minister and the two subsequently had an affair. It was then that she became pregnant with my sister, Karen, who is one year older than me. My sister, Jackie, is two years older than me, and Jenna is four years younger. Once my mother got pregnant and carried a baby to term successfully, she had not been able to "turn off" the "baby machine," she said.

We were all, needless to say, more than shocked at Mother's confession. Apparently, my birth father had known that baby Karen was not his but Oliver's. It is my firm belief that my birth father, knowing that the baby wasn't his, never really loved my sister Karen. Nothing she did, or tried to do, ever earned his love, that critical paternal love. I believe that to this day this may be the primary reason that she has difficulty with relationships with men. Unfortunately, that was the fabric of her childhood and her most crucial father-daughter relationship.

Worse yet, my mother overly favored Karen. We had all seen that. Now, Mother told us why. Karen was, in her own words, her "love child," her special one. Karen was in essence a living reminder of this wonderful love affair and tender time she spent with a man whom she adored. Remarkably, my mother never lost the deep love and respect she had for him, this minister who cheated on his wife, fathered an illegitimate child and, in his final act, ended his own life by suicide. He killed himself, Mother related, due to his guilt. This was my sister's birth father, this preacher, a hypocritical man of God.

Years and years ago, I remember my birth father telling me disgustedly that a big part of his problem with my mother had been that Mother believed that she was beyond shame, above reproach, because she truly believed that she had, in essence, been sanctified because she had "slept with the church."

At the time, it hadn't made a bit of sense to me and Father would say no more. It remained one of those unexplained things that one files away in one's mind under "this makes no sense." That is, until now. Now, I see. At long last, I understand.

I find it odd that my mother doesn't view her immoral actions as worthy of shame. It was simply wrong, having a baby with another woman's husband. Yet, she looks back on it as a romantic and semi-holy event. She sees her love child as more than human and treats her accordingly.

Nonetheless, I must state for the record that I am and will always be extremely and utterly grateful that I was not that love child, that "special one." Perhaps Mother's obsession with Karen helps to explain, at least in part, the migraine headaches my sister has experienced her entire adult life.

Of course, I also now understand the horseback riding lessons that Karen received as a child that I did not, and the semester at an expensive college that Karen received that I did not. It is good, at long last, to at least now know the reason why and to know that it had nothing whatsoever to do with anything I ever did or did not do.

Tuesday, January 4, 2000: My ex-husband's sister, Melissa's first child, Benjamin, is born: seven pounds, one ounce. Mother and son are doing fine.

Melissa doesn't call me right away, as she is busy with the birth and all, but she is calling me from the hospital with the last of her calling card minutes. I am the ONLY one coming down to help her out, but it seems the last one on her list to call. How odd.

Wednesday, January 5, 2000: How rotten I feel. When I went to my counselor today (I like to call her "Greenie") and shared with her my plans regarding going down to Florida to help my ex-husband's sister, Melissa, (who has remained close despite the divorce) with her new baby, Greenie said, "And just how is it going to be good for you — to go to Florida, to fall in love with THIS baby, and then have to give it up, too? Just how is that going to be good for YOU?"

I replied, "But I promised her I would be there. She has to have this foot operation, and I TOLD her I would come and she is depending on me! She asked ME to come, and I HAVE to go!"

Greenie pointed out that Melissa has a husband, and that's what husbands are for, to take care of their wives and family. Moreover, when one is deep in therapy, working on issues, important issues, one does not need to complicate matters.

It makes sense. I have to trust her judgment. I want SO MUCH to get my hands on that baby. It's been almost twenty years since my last pregnancy and my miscarriage — since I lost the twins — and I've never had that deep yearning for another baby even partially satisfied.

"Tell her right away," she advised, "the sooner, the better. Tell her tonight!"

When I called, Melissa was still in the hospital, enjoying the second day of her firstborn baby's life. While I hated myself for telling her that I could not come, I told her exactly what my counselor had said, and Melissa seemed to understand. I sure do not want to hurt our relationship. She seemed to understand but she must be in partial shock and also really devastated that I'd do this at this late date. What a rotten thing to do to someone who has just had her first baby. To put this kind of damper on her joy seems simply rotten. I'm sick about it.

One positive thing though — we did straighten something out. She pointed out that I should have never volunteered to come down in the first place. I reminded her that she had ASKED me to come down to help her out. I did not "volunteer." I was asked, and I was willing to give her a week of my vacation time from work because I love her like a daughter. But I had absolutely not volunteered to do so. (In reality, my husband had been adamantly against it from the start.)

She answered that she had asked me because she did not trust her Aunt Amelia. She said that there was NO ONE else whom she trusted who could or would come, and so, she had asked me. At that time, although I felt that I could not say "no" to her, I actually did not "volunteer."

This is good — that it was clarified exactly who was helping whom in this instance. Tomas was right. Sometimes, people in Florida think that it's a privilege to come down to visit them. Meanwhile, Tomas and I are giving up our winter vacation time together, at Mother and Dad's condo in Florida, which is where we would have gone had I not been going down alone to help Melissa. (Of course, I did not tell Melissa that.)

Thursday, January 6, 2000: Did I do the right thing? Have I made a huge mistake? I'm afraid to call Melissa because I'm afraid she will be mad. The more I think about it and how cold the winter weather is getting, and the more I am realizing how much I was looking forward to holding that baby and helping my friend, the more I am so furious with myself that I took Greenie's advice and decided NOT to go to Florida.

I am going to try to make it right. I got up my courage and called Melissa, to see what she has worked out. Surely, she can still get Aunt Amelia. She tells me that Aunt Amelia's on medication and that she can't trust her. I know now that Melissa is stuck but she's too angry with me to even consider having me come now. She tries not to sound mad, saying that she understands, but I can hear that she is so hurt, but still determined — she says she'll manage though she still doesn't know how. I'm going to send her a letter.

Thursday, January 13, 2000: I sent a loving letter today by Federal Express, overnight, so that Melissa will not be worrying one second longer than necessary. I feel so awful.

Friday, January 14, 2000: Haven't heard from Melissa yet. I'm wondering if she even got the letter. I cannot call her. I must wait for her to call me.

Saturday, January 15, 2000: Still no word. I want to call her, but I know I must wait for her to respond to me.

Sunday, January 16, 2000: Finally, she called (of course, during the ONE television show I love to watch all week — *Star Trek Voyager*)! She was so touched by my letter, and best of all, she wants me to come. I am going!! Hooray!!

Wednesday, February 9, 2000: I can't believe it! Today is the day! I fly to Florida today — into the summer and into the warmth and love surrounding a precious newborn. I can hardly wait! If they knew how much I wanted to get my hands on the baby, they'd never let me NEAR him! I carried and lost my twin boys so long ago. But the pain and grief make it feel like it was only yesterday. Soon, I will at long last have a baby in my yearning arms. Off I go, to Florida.

Wednesday, February 9, 2000, Evening: Melissa and I stayed up talking until 2:30 a.m. Good thing I had ten hours of sleep last night. But now, I see I am going to become as sleep deprived as I see that she is. She seems so tired and so down and she's changed so much. I'm glad that I came down a day early, a day before her foot surgery, to get the hang of her "routine" as I can see she wants things done EXACTLY her way. I do want to not only be a help but would like to also please her and be a comfort as best I can. I absolutely cannot get enough of holding tiny Ben. I adore the way he coos and smiles as I cuddle him in my arms.

Thursday, February 10, 2000: We spent the day going over the bottle routine, taking care of Ben, and getting ready for tomorrow's surgery, which is early a.m. Ben is having trouble moving his bowels. Melissa gave him three doses of prune juice today.

Melissa told me today that I am driving her to the hospital in the morning, then waiting until she goes in for surgery, then coming home with Ben while she is in recovery and then coming back later to get her. Although I wondered why her husband, Duncan, can't at least take her in the morning and save Ben and me from having to go out twice, I'm not going to make any waves or question her plan. Duncan is so good with Ben and working so hard and he looks very thin and terribly overworked. I will manage.

Friday, February 11, 2000: Melissa was furious with Duncan that his vehicle was parked in front of hers in the early a.m. when it was time for us three to head to the hospital. He got up and moved it, and off we went. He just didn't think ahead.

Finally, when Ben and I got home, I was at last alone with the baby and could really enjoy him. No hovering new mother, breathing down my neck, telling me exactly what to do. HE IS SO ADORABLE! I enjoyed rocking him and laid him down after I rocked him to sleep. A little later, I heard a tiny whimper from him. I tiptoed into the room, saw his eyes were closed, and reached out for him in a loving gesture (but did not touch him). He reached out (in his sleep) and gave a little shudder, like he was okay as long as he could sense that he wasn't alone. Then, he went back to sleep. He is so precious; I love him so much. It is so WONDERFUL to have him all to myself. I am SO GOOD WITH HIM. He loves me, too. He's a good baby.

My mother and dad, who have been snowbirds for several years, asked to come for a short visit today to see the new baby. They always liked Melissa and since they're nearby, I thought it might be nice for Melissa, too. Since she had said it'd be fine, I decided to make a special dinner for their visit, my homemade meatloaf.

Although I'd decided to make a nice dinner today, the baby had had too much prune juice the day before and was keeping me busy either changing diapers or comforting him.

After I brought Melissa home from the hospital, all hell broke loose. Trying to care for two hurting "babies" was absolutely exhausting. I couldn't even find ten minutes to throw the meatloaf together and put it in the oven. At 3:00 p.m., when Mother and Dad arrived, I THANKED GOD they were here, and Mother immediately chipped in and started helping, mainly trying to calm the extremely irritated (from too much prune juice) baby.

I managed to get the meatloaf made, but by the time Duncan got home, I was so glad to see him that I could've cried. He took charge of Ben, and Mother was able to help me with the dinner and the bottles and taking care of Melissa, post foot surgery.

Later, in the kitchen, Mother said to me, "I see there's a little something between you and Duncan."

Blown away, I did not answer right then except to deny it, stating that he is so good with the baby, I was just glad to see him get home to help.

"There's no attraction there!" I tell her. She gazed out the kitchen window in a wistful, dreamy way and replied, "Ahhh, yes, that's how it started for me!"

Later, thinking about it, I was furious. I got her alone and said, "Mother, I want you to know something — I never cheated on my first husband, and I never cheated on my second husband, and I never will. There is NOTHING between Duncan and me. That is YOUR trip, NOT MINE!"

But later at dinner, when she was sitting next to Duncan enjoying the meatloaf I had made, Mother said, "Susie is such a *won-der-ful* cook, isn't she, Duncan?" in a tone that was lost on all those present but me.

Saturday, February 12, 2000: In the evening, when we were all sitting around, Mother asked for a foot rub. I'm something of an amateur masseuse and know the positive effects of any type of massage. So, I was giving Mother a relaxing foot rub, and Duncan sat down next to her.

She said to him (after a few other words), LAUGHINGLY and teasingly, "Oh, I thought you were in line to be next!"

This embarrassed me tremendously.

Melissa spoke up, and volunteered, "Oh, I haven't given Duncan a foot rub in a long time."

Mother was constantly implying that there was possibly something inappropriate between Duncan and me, and of course, there wasn't. But it has totally weirded out the whole trip for me and definitely hindered the way I related to my dear friend's husband with whom I <u>must</u> work to coordinate the care of both Melissa and baby Ben. Add to that the fact that Mother without hesitation let me sleep on the floor, with my back as bad as it had now been feeling, even though she had an offer from nearby friends in this same neighborhood to stay in their guest bedroom!!

Knowing that my back was giving me pain, she had turned their invitation down, not caring one bit about my back and the fact that I would have to sleep on the floor, thus making my back pain even worse. Their friends were only a few blocks away and actually I would have gladly stayed there myself, but unfortunately, they have cats. I am severely allergic to cats, so it was out of the question for me.

Monday: February 14, 2000: I cannot believe that it seems like an entire LIFETIME that I have been gone, when it has been only five days. I am in this very timeless place, where time seems to be moving so very, very slowly.

I have decided not to tell my husband, Tomas, anything that went on in Florida about Mother's verbal implications regarding Duncan and me as Tomas will undoubtedly get furious. I sleep most of the way home, on the two airplane flights, as I am so utterly exhausted and so totally disoriented that I barely know where or who I am. After I land and we are waiting for the baggage though, I feel so safe and so happy to be back in his arms that I begin to tell my husband how utterly horrid it was down there, what Mother implied, and how totally out of line it all was, and yes, he gets very, very angry. His anger sparks something in me — a feeling of validation, of protection, of (thank God) SOMEONE believing in me, in my goodness, and in my honor.

After we are in the car and on the way home from the airport, we are still discussing it, when it hits me — in Florida, Mother was actually throwing me at Duncan, just the exact same way that she threw me at my father — at my own father!!!!!! She more or less pushed us towards him in inappropriate ways while approving some of father's inappropriate actions. She hid from him by hiding behind us, especially my oldest sister, when he was drunk, allowing him to fawn over her in sickening ways that weren't comfortable or appropriate!!

I am furious. I am pounding on the dashboard and screaming, "She THREW me at my father! ! ! ! ! She f#@!!!ing threw US at our father ! ! ! ! !"

I am sick. I am furious. I cannot believe it. Poor Tomas is trying to drive, trying to understand. It is after one o'clock in the morning by the time we get home, both numb. He decides to try to go to work the next day, but I know I will not.

Tuesday, February 15, 2000: I was never so glad to be in my own, safe house in my entire life. I awoke feeling as if in a dream, totally disoriented and weak and starving. (I lost five pounds in the five days I was in Florida, on what turned out to also be Mother's trip down memory lane.)

I do my morning necessities and am eventually a little chilly, so I decide to heat my corn pouch in the microwave. I hold it in my left arm, close to me, warming me, as I wander through my wonderful house, looking and looking, and just being. As I am wandering, for some reason I am touching my lips with my right hand, and I wander into my step-daughter Katy's room. Such beautiful things grace the walls, such spiritual things. And then I see the stained-glass picture by the door and I realize that her room feels sacred, like a church. I am totally and completely safe here.

As I am looking up and feeling safe, I become aware that I am rubbing my lips and I wonder why am I rubbing my lips like this, and I realize, as I hold my warmed pouch in my left arm (like a little girl holding a teddy bear) and rubbing my lips with my right-hand fingers, that I am/was a very little girl who was kissed very violently and very improperly by her daddy and whose lips hurt, and she is rubbing them to try to soothe them and make them feel better as she wanders through the house, not knowing where to go, not having anywhere to go or anyone to turn to for help.

I cry as I remember, and I run to the phone and call my husband and tell him what I remember! It is a eureka moment for me as I remember that my daddy KISSED me badly, and I am crying. My husband says that it is alright, and he makes me feel better and safe again. I am so lucky that I have him to protect me now.

February 16, 2000: It is not bad getting back to work, though I feel like I am such a different person, and I just want to SHOUT to everyone: "I was MOLESTED as a child!!!! I have JUST only NOW remembered it!"

It is difficult to keep my mouth shut, but it seems wisest NOT to say anything right now. I did tell my sisters, both Jackie and Karen who have known for their whole adult lives that they were molested by him. Jackie was wonderful and said, among other things, "You are strong enough now to handle this — you would not have remembered otherwise. You are going to be fine; I'm sending some tapes that will help you."

She was supportive and loving. I have decided to wait until I see Karen in person to tell her, this weekend. (As Jackie lives in another city, I had to tell her over the phone, but I prefer to relate something this shocking to Karen in person.)

Thursday, February 17, 2000: Getting back into the routine of work was good for me. It seems to have helped me to somewhat get over the initial shock of being a victim of incest. My main focus now is JOY at remembering the child named Susie!!!! I see her in my mind's eye with this big, round, soft, adorable head full of hair. She is so soft and cuddly and innocent and very loving and definitely fun-loving. She loves just everyone and is so much fun and has boundless energy and is just the most beautiful being that I have ever imagined.

I love her so much. I remember how she used to wear her hair, and I am wearing it like that all the time. I REMEMBER her, and I marvel that I had ever forgotten her at all. It is so, so wonderful, remembering her. It's like meeting up with the most wonderful person in your past that you totally and completely forgot about, almost like a miracle, and it's the most exciting, joyful thing. I just want to PLAY, and I want Jackie and Karen to PLAY and to remember and to have a good time together and just be kids again. We had so much FUN together as kids, at times.

After all, for me, being KISSED is not so bad. Also, it was so long ago. When I want, I can really distance myself from it all, as I am, after all, quite a successful, healthy and vibrant woman now. My husband, Tomas, has been so perfect, treating me like a fragile egg. He wouldn't even try to kiss me or anything or to force himself upon me in any way, shape, or form. A perfect gentleman he is, that one, and perfectly loving, also. I don't deserve him. He loves me so much. I can see it, now. I never knew he REALLY loved me. I hope he loves little Susie, too, because she's what I want to be, forever and ever. Now that I have her back, I NEVER want to lose my inner child again.

I am in shock, though, still, that I could have forgotten her at all. I feel like I am not a REAL person, but one who has been asleep all her life and is just waking up, and it's so strange, it's so all-consuming and I know I am so emotional, and I know Tomas fears I am going nuts.

Friday, February 18, 2000: My first appointment with a hypnotherapist is today. What an act of providence. The forces that be, the Divine forces, definitely led me to her. I discovered her yesterday, and we talked yesterday, and to her surprise, she had an opening today for me at 4:00. Thank heaven!

I need someone to speak with so much, and someone who can help unlock the rest of my mind. Amazingly, she is in Madison Shops. How incredible! In my childhood, Mother was always going to and talking about Madison Shops, Madison Shops. It was one of her favorite places to shop. Now, it is close to home for me, also, and is a very important place for me, too.

After my first session, I find I really like Dr. Maribeth Hart. She is very kind and loving and when she plays/acts like a little girl, I LOVE her little girl. We don't do any hypnotherapy but discuss my memories and other things. She has a joyful playfulness and can giggle, and she gets me giggling. Today, she gave me delicious cookies to eat, my favorite — pizzelles!

Saturday, February 19, 2000: I got up today, excited about telling my sister Karen about the breakthrough in my memory! I took her to McMurphy's today, shopping, telling her the story of my visit to Florida. I visited with her for hours afterward, talking and crying together. She showed me her "Wild Hearts" book that she'd found, after a lifetime of searching, and amazingly, I have found my "Snow Queen" movie, also after a lifetime of searching for this childhood treasure. Each of these reminds us of our respective childhoods.

Sunday, February 20, 2000: I am lying in bed in the a.m., doing my "ahhhh" meditation, and I am so relaxed, contented, my meditation so deep that it puts me into a self-hypnotic state, actually. I have the second appointment with my hypnotherapist next week. I am looking forward to it, and this a.m., I find myself curious and adventurous as through the meditation I slip myself into a semi-hypnotic state.

I am a little girl, watching a scene unfold. My mother and father are at the baby changing table. Mother is on the right, Father on the left, with the baby sort of between them, and they are both marveling over her beauty and it is a tender scene until in the course of their discussion, the tone changes as Mother says:

"Carl, you're VIOLATING the three older girls! You HAVE to stop it!"

He retorts something about her not being able to stop him, and the baby gets dragged into the conversation, and he says something like, "You think I can't????"

My mother is fighting him, physically, trying to stop him from hurting the baby. He is doing something to the baby and the baby is screaming and Mother is screaming and that is all that I know. I do not see what happens to the baby, but I immediately come back to the present, get up out of my bed, and run to tell someone what I have just remembered, as I am very excited to remember.

It is very important, and wanting to tell the two people closest to me at the same time, I telephone Karen though I know she is asleep, and I tell her and Tomas at the same time what I have remembered. Neither, of course, shares my excitement over this ugly remembrance, and both, I imagine, think I am a little nuts for being EXCITED about remembering. It is SUCH a feat for my mind to unlock! But no one can know the JOY of this but me, I can see.

Tomas and I went to church today, but we did not share with anyone what has happened. They were all surprised to see me back early from Florida, but I did not get a chance to really talk to anyone.

Wednesday, February 23, 2000: At the hypnotherapist's office, she does put me in a trance, as I am CURIOUS to know what happened to me. I have had a dream about a belt, a big, wide belt, and I don't know what it means. I know I'll never know what happened to the baby, as I could not see it (Mother's and Father's bodies were blocking my line of vision). But what did Father do to ME?

She puts me under and it comes out — more of the scene at the baby's changing table unfolds. After the horrid act, whatever it was, Father said, "Now look what we've done!"

Mother answered, with death in her voice, "What do you mean, WE?"

Then, they both gasp as they see me! They realize Susie is there.

"Susie saw!!!! What are we going to do now?"

Father comes at me, from my left, with this evil look on his face, and he puts his fingers over my nose, pinching it, and puts his hand over my mouth, smothering me, suffocating me.

. . . *the worst abuse* . . .

The therapist JUMPS in horror as I relate this and she touches me, stroking my arm, telling me it's alright as she brings me out.

I am in shock. So is she. He tried to kill me and (I assume) my mother stopped him.

Friday, February 25, 2000: I barely know day to day what I am doing. Ever since I flew to Florida,

I have been in this extremely TIMELESS place. It seems like EONS have passed since February 15th when I first remembered the sexual abuse and now I remember so much more.

My husband is pulling me along through life these days, to work, to the gym, to the store, to eat, here and there. I know I would not be moving along without him, and it is enough that I let him lead me, much in the same way that Jackie and Karen led little Susie for her entire childhood. I was just a little tag-along, like a kite on the wind, trailing happily after the other two.

And poor Jenna, she wanted to go too, but she was too little. She often had to be left behind, which she remembers to this day. She was so left out that once she became a mother, she would never EVER let her older child, a boy, do anything the younger one, a girl, could not. They were years apart and so it was not appropriate that she was as extreme about this as she was, causing the older child tremendous resentments. To this day, Jenna claims that she feels left out, left behind, and out of the loop, regardless of whether in actuality she is or is not.

But as for me, back then, I usually did get to go along with the older sisters to play unsupervised, and I had fun, too.

Now, though, sometimes I feel I am in shock, and I don't know what will happen, and I am afraid. I feel the terror of my childhood, as well as the joy, and I don't want to slip into a depression.

Saturday, February 26, 2000: I REMEMBER now. I remembered what happened. It was so rough on me, the hypnotherapy. It gave me such a headache. I'd thought I'd rather hypnotize myself. I did my meditation again in the morning and remembered that, after the baby screamed, after Mother screamed, after Father finally walked away from the table and Mother started comforting the baby, she said, in surprise:

"The baby's BLEEDING! You broke her 'high man,' Carl."

Carl came over, pushed her aside, not believing, to see for himself. It must have been at that point that he said, looking down and falling back, "Look what we've done now" to which my mother replied, "What do you mean, WE?"

When they saw me, he tried to get rid of one witness to the horrendous thing he had just done.

After that day, he repeatedly tried to (seemingly accidentally) kill me, and I lived in mortal terror for my life. Jackie did protect me, as did others at times. But he would joke about it, trying to push me off the edge of something, teasing about hurting me, hurting me, teasing more and enjoying it, even laughing about it. He set my hair on fire once, tossing lit matches at me. He dragged me sound asleep down wooden steps by my feet, my head bouncing off every step.

Saturday, February 26, 2000 (later that day): Worst of all, because I decided that rather than telling

119

Jackie and Karen any more memories, I thought I would suggest to Jackie that she try to remember about the "high man," so we could compare notes. Maybe she could at her hypnotherapist remember for herself when we tried to find out what the "high man" was. Then, if she remembered the same thing, we would be dead certain about it. (That is, it would actually "prove" that the events did indeed occur).

We were curious as girls about something we did not understand (the "high man") and I would think that that curiosity does not give up easily and would possibly be an accessible though suppressed memory. But when I suggested such to Jackie, she became infuriated! She would not, no — could not — she said, validate my memories.

I wanted Jackie to remember the high man question, as surely the mind would remember something that went UNEXPLAINED, something about which it wondered. But Jackie got really mad at me because I suggested she might want to remember anything more about our childhood. She has suffered enough.

She told me so in a nasty email that I hated because she made me remember that Jackie and Karen did not LIKE Susie, the girl that I once was and who, until now, was perfect in my mind's eye. Susie was a big-mouth, loose cannon who never knew when to keep her mouth shut — never COULD keep her mouth shut and this caused a lot of trouble for everyone.

The other girls did not trust her, nor did they really like her. I wet the bed most nights. I was the "Peetail." And I stunk like pee. And I sucked my thumb. And I was not all peaches and cream and damn Jackie to hell for not letting me totally love that "perfect" little girl just a little bit longer before reminding me of who she REALLY was!

My memory is:

I asked Jackie, "Jackie, what's a HIGH man?"

Jackie replied, "I don't know – why?"

I can see her as clearly as if it were yesterday!

I said, "Because Daddy broke the baby's HIGH man and I want to know what it is."

As we both didn't know, she picked a good moment when mommy was cooking dinner in the kitchen and things were calm, to casually ask Mother what a high man was.

Mother said, "Carl, the girls are wondering what a HIGH man is."

Father told us that it is a very bad word that little girls are never to say again, and Susie said, loud and clear and strong, "high man high man high man high man" as if to say, *you're not going to shut me up*!

Then, Father got scotch tape and taped her mouth shut, which was very tight and was on for a long, long time, and which he roughly removed, and it was, I think, after he tore it off that he kissed me, violently, digging his unshaven rough jimmies into my skin, hurting me, scaring me. It was that that I had originally re-remembered.

February 26, 2000: Now I realize WHY Jackie no longer desires to remember. Today while meditating, I reflected (for some reason) back to when I first made love, when I first had intercourse, and I wondered, *was there any blood??!! Oh, God, was there no blood?!*

I DON'T want to tell my therapist. It may have not been just a kiss that happened to me at my father's hands. I believe I left my body a lot as a child. The good forces (my "higher self"?) took me away, shut me down, kept me from experiencing the violence that was happening, like when my head was banging on the steps as he dragged me down the long, wooden staircase.

I only know about that because Jackie has told me about it. I was asleep at the time. Bless them. **I thank God I have been blessed this long with NOT KNOWING and not remembering all of this.** It was long enough to have grown some self-esteem and self-love and inner strength that are serving me well right now.

Sunday, February 27, 2000: Today, at church, I cried during the first hymn. Fortunately, I was in the back of the church with my dear neighbors, Mr. and Mrs. Kingston, who were very kind although they had no idea of why I was crying.

On the way out, Reverend Nathan Johnston casually asked me, "What do you know?"

As most everyone had left the vestibule by then,

I took it literally and answered, "What do I KNOW? What do I KNOW? Do you really want to KNOW what I KNOW!!???!! I know the most evil and horrible thing, and I would love to tell you . . . "

There, in the vestibule, with Mrs. Kingston hugging me as needed, I made a "confession" of sorts to Pastor Johnston, and to Mr. and Mrs. Kingston. I told them EVERYTHING as I cried.

They were shocked. But they were wonderful.

Pastor Johnston said, among many other things, "You must pray for your mother. It is important she starts facing these things here, in this life."

He also said something else very important. He said that this is my opportunity, now that I am so weak, to let God be my strength. Not my husband, not myself, not anyone but God. And I am. I am.

After I left church and was driving home, I was so glad that I had shared my story with them, for now I have a plan. I will invite Mother to go to that church with me when she returns.

I spent much of this day paralyzed, unable to move, unable to clean or do anything but cry and cry and cry. Today I felt my pain; today it came out.

Monday, February 28, 2000: During my session after work today with my therapist, Maribeth, instead of focusing on the past, we focused on the future, as my son, Lee, is coming over tomorrow to move his possessions into his new apartment and I want to reconnect with him so badly, and I want to get together a plan on how to do it. I love him so much.

She gave me ideas and suggestions, and she has somehow put me back on a POSITIVE path, thank God! I did NOT tell her what I remembered about there possibly being no blood for me the first intercourse time. We did not do any hypnotherapy.

After getting home, I took her advice and told Tomas that he did not have to be here when Lee comes tomorrow to move, as I want to try to make it a positive reconnection. Tomas is very, very angry and although I am afraid, I am being very courageous and doing what is true to my soul! I decided to share with him what I had written in Lee's baby book after he was born. I actually wrote extra pages and placed them lovingly within the journal. I read the whole story aloud to Tomas, actually. What a wonderful, fabulous trip down memory lane. I WAS a wonderful mother and now, I know that my obsession with babies actually began with my love for my sweet sister, baby Jenna!

Tuesday, February 29, 2000: Tonight, I did a loving thing in being kind to my ex-husband. I was also totally loving and connected with my Lee!!!! YAY!!!

After Lee moved his stuff over, with his dad's help, to his new apartment, I went with Lee to Mattress World to buy him a nice bed, something I have wanted to do forever and something which was extremely satisfying. After a teenage growth spurt, he needed an extra-long bed (so his feet would not hang off), and we couldn't afford it back then. Now, I can afford it.

We sat outside Mattress World and talked. There, I told my story to the one person (the ONLY person really) who always KNEW something was extremely wrong with my person even before I suspected anything. Yes, he was the ONLY one who knew that I was not a "real" person — my Lee.

Upon hearing my story, he was not the least bit surprised. He knew all along that something was very, very wrong. He had said to my mother a long time ago, "Grandma, my mom is TOO happy!"

My mother had related it to me, saying it to illustrate that something was wrong with Lee that he thought that. She had made me promise to never tell him that she had told me and broken his confidence. But now, it makes sense. I WAS "too happy" and Lee was the only one who not only saw it, but who knew that something was very askew underneath.

I was also dying to tell Lee because he has a right to know what made me, his mother, what she has been and continues to be today. All of this impacted his life, albeit undoubtedly on a subconscious as well as conscious level. He has a right to the truth, as does his brother Jack.

Lee was not surprised, though he was shocked and angry. He was loving and understanding. The next day, on the phone, as he thanked me for buying the bed, I heard such love in his voice. It was like cool water to someone who had been in the sun on the desert for weeks and weeks, dying of thirst, to hear that my son knows how much I love him, to hear it in his voice that he feels loved. That makes me feel totally content.

I also heard in his voice the love that he feels, too, for me. Yet, I feel such guilt that I failed to protect him from the hell that he has been through these past years. He was a very "special" child, advanced, we were told. In hindsight, I'd say he was too smart for his own good.

I wish I could have afforded a higher quality school for him. I wish I could have nurtured and challenged and guided that sensitive mind into a positive, fulfilling direction. I know that blaming myself is pointless. I know that I have to keep my focus on the positives and on the future, not the past. He IS turning his life around and God is at work here, also. It's not all on my shoulders.

March 1, 2000: I was strong and brave yesterday. I told Tomas that it is my house, too, and that his negative, judgmental vibes are not welcome around my son, Lee.

It was a huge step, and today, I am amazed that it is March 1st. It was on March 1st, 1985, that I stepped away from Peter and separated from my first husband. I have indeed, in a sense, stepped away from Tomas. I refuse to turn my back on my son, on my wonderful son, Lee. I refuse to stop loving him; and I refuse to be untrue to myself.

March 2, 2000: I realized today, walking down the steps at work: that they are JUST MEMORIES!!!! Up until this moment, from February 15, 2000, when I first remembered, to March 1, 2000, I had been LIVING IT. It had been real. I had been as immersed in it as if it had been last week.

I am now ASTOUNDED that I only now realize that they are JUST MEMORIES. Moreover, these memories exist in my mind only. I am alone with these memories.

They are not here and now, but then and gone. They are powerful but they are yesterday's.

I realize something else today. In remembering, I am victorious. I HAVE WON. Curses on you, Carl Stephens!!!! You thought you locked it away in that little girl's head forever and ever and ever and YOU DIDN'T! I WON!!

I remember! I remember! Wherever your spirit may be, I KNOW you know, and I want the whole WORLD to know what you so desperately tried to hide. I remember Mother telling us girls that:

"You know, a girl can sometimes rupture her hymen by vigorous exercise, and you girls are all SO active . . . "

I remember her telling us that now. I suspect in a corner of my mind that there is more about her that I will be remembering.

March 3, 2000: It does seem that Carl did a good job on MY head, though, I must admit. He confused me totally and completely. He terrorized me, also. On many levels, I have no desire to live in a world with men. But I suspect as I remember more of Mother, I may soon feel the same way about women as well.

If I could move to France today and live with French-speaking people, I would do it in a heartbeat. I began studying French in the third grade when I was just eight years old and was inducted into the advanced scholars' program at school. I fell in love with the beautiful French language so much that I studied it every year and have continued to do so throughout my college years. I have so much French in my head, just screaming to come out, just wanting to emerge.

When I speak the French, you see, my body language is ONE with my intentions and with my words, and I am a DIFFERENT person. I feel like a beautiful and sensuous, yet innocent woman and I love French so much. Here, I am not finding someone with whom to speak it, and I need to. I NEED to.

I RESOLVED a day or so ago that Carl Stephens has terrorized me enough. He has negatively impacted enough of my life. I REFUSE to let him hurt me anymore. I resolve to be in the here and now, to enjoy and thrive during the remainder of my life. I will not be controlled by the monsters and terrors of the past that I now remember. If I am controlled, he wins. If I heal, I win.

I AM determined to win.

And I live to see my sisters win, also! I will do whatever is within my power to move in that direction, including telling my therapist what I fear about a lack of blood when I lost my virginity and including undergoing hypnotherapy to bring out the rest of the truth. I do hope the worst is already known.

My poor Tomas — at first (Feb. 15th forward), he was the hero in my story, and somewhere along the line, he transformed into one of the enemies in my mind.

Tonight, we decided to start sleeping in the same bed together again. I have been so self-absorbed. It's time to start caring about those whom I love, to wake up and see those around me who need my love as much as I need theirs.

I want to run and hide, and Lord, I cannot believe I must get a new full-time job at this gut-wrenching time in my life, but I started looking this week, trusting that I will find that right place for me.

Gratitude is what I feel in some ways. I pray for my Lee. I grieve for what he has gone through. Help me to keep my focus on LOVING him, dear Lord. Thank you for carrying me through these times.

Thank you for sending my long-time gym buddy, Joel, to me today at the gym. I told him I felt like I was losing my mind because of something that's happened. He advised that I write it all down, get it all out, on paper. It was he who inspired me to come home and write my diary, from the beginning of remembering to this point right here. I've been aching to write all along and wish I had been writing as I went.

Know that I have cried and cried tonight, writing these four hours, all of this. Thank YOU for all the "coincidences" that have brought me exactly where I am right now, from NOT calling my friend, Sheila, while down in Florida, and perhaps prolonging my Florida visit, to a loving Melissa and loving Katy, without both of whom I would not have remembered what I did.

Oh — I also remembered after rereading this tonight, sharing it with Tomas and talking, that Dad Stephens beat me many times, probably within inches of my life, and tortured the others when they had to watch the beatings. I was perhaps the luckiest one in that situation, because I left my body, I am sure, and was spared the agony that the others felt, watching me suffer and being unable to stop him.

Also, I (and Tomas) CANNOT BELIEVE it's only been a few short weeks that have passed since this all began. It seems like an eternity — to BOTH of us. I suspect we are not out of the nightmare yet and that the past is still controlling both of us more than we'd like to know.

March 4, 2000: Well, I had a bad night's sleep last night. Tomas woke me up two times with his snoring, and when I awoke at 4:00 a.m., I never did get back to sleep, thinking, thinking, thinking about Lee.

I couldn't stop worrying.

Then, I did the "ahhhhh" meditation and found my way back to some peace. Now, we have meditated together, and I am planning this morning on cleaning, taking care of some paperwork, and trying to keep my focus positive.

Tomas and I had a good talk this morning. I realize he has absolutely no idea of how totally drained I am, from crying last night so much and then not sleeping well, though the poor dear tells me he did not sleep a wink almost every night this week, worrying about me (and about us, our marriage, I imagine, though he did not say that).

I think he is beginning to GET that it will not help Lee to be reminded of how he has been stumbling these past years, that what he needs is support in keeping his focus on moving forward, on the positive, and what he CAN do, not on what he has done wrong.

The same goes for me, I'm sure. I'm grateful for this beautiful day and the sunshine. My prayer for today is that Love can speak through me, that the words that will come out of me will be ones of Love and Compassion, not of judgment and blaming. I hope to pause and think before I speak and to maintain this feeling of peace and well-being that has been planted in me despite feeling drained.

Sunday, March 5, 2000: Last week at church, as I already noted, on my way out, Pastor Johnston had looked at me and said, "What do you know?"

I had been upset during the service, crying a bit, and when he said that, most everyone was out of the church already, and so I had looked at him and had replied:

"What do I KNOW? What do I KNOW? Do you want to KNOW what I KNOW?"

Then, I told him everything, all of it, amidst tears and horror, amidst being held by Mrs. Kingston with Mr. Kingston standing off a bit, also listening and looking as if he were in shock. They were perfect. All of them were actually, utterly perfect in the way that they responded to me. They were sympathetic and loving, shocked yet understanding and caring and compassionate. None of them doubted my truth and none of them thought the less of me for it, I know.

Pastor Johnston said that this is my opportunity now, to allow God, to truly allow God and God alone to be my strength, now that I am so weak. He said, not your husband, not yourself, nothing but God, allow him to be your strength. I also heard him say, "Pray for your mother. It is important that, in this lifetime, she deals with all of this."

Well, I talked to them last week for probably a good half hour, and they comforted and loved me more than words can say, and they upheld me, and I knew, all week, that they were praying for me.

I was so looking forward to going to church today but also wondering, too, how they would all act towards me now, now that they know. When

Tomas and I walked into that church (the service had already begun), I saw a beaming smile break out on Pastor Johnston's face, and Mr. Kingston motioned for us to come and sit with him and Helene and Don (but there really wasn't room, so we sat a few rows ahead).

The service was about LOVE, about how God loved us FIRST and that is how we know we can trust him. I love that church. After the service, Pastor Johnston looked me in the eyes on my way out and said how deeply glad he was to see me there today. Mr. Kingston talked with us a bit, and Irma Harner was there. Wonderful Irma came and asked me how I was. Mrs. Kingston (who was not present due to being ill) had shared the whole story with Irma, who said she had been so worried about me.

When I got home, I felt awful, realizing how worried they all must have been all week, and I called Pastor Johnston and apologized for worrying them so and thanked him, too. He warned me that, although I told him I was feeling very much at peace today, the anger would return.

I had a wonderful Sunday, making love later on with Tomas (only the third time since I've remembered, and not the best of the three times either, but it had been so long since the last time, and we were both in ways desperate for release which put a pressure on of sorts).

Also, as we went into it, I remembered what I had once learned in psychology, that when two people make love, there are actually six people in that bed, the man, the woman, his mother and father, and her mother and father, in an underlying subconscious sense.

Hmmmm, for me, that would mean that there is a monster in the bed. Not a good thought, and not one, of course, that I shared with Tomas.

I did NOT think French, and that was the difference between the last two times we made love, when I WAS the French woman. I think I shall think French from now on when making love!

We went to the home of our friends, Mick and Martha, for a wonderful supper (stuffed pasta shells, garlic bread, and salad) and lots of conversation and laughter.

Monday, March 6, 2000: Thank God for angels like Reverend Nathan Johnston. I found myself quite angry today, and when I remembered Reverend Johnston's warning of yesterday, it somehow made the anger "okay" since it is to be expected. I got angry thinking about Mick's family and how lucky those girls are and it angers me that mine was what it was.

I talked to Karen today and learned that Jenna's husband, Chester, went on a cruise without Jenna, that Karen spent yesterday with her boyfriend, Rick, and neither of those was good to hear. I feel strong today though. I feel "grown up" in some ways, and I am determined to move ahead with getting another full-time job.

Tomorrow is the hypnotherapist session. I must confess I am a little afraid. I suppose I must tell her what I now suspect about the first time I ever made love — that is, that there may not have been any blood afterwards and no evidence of virginity.

Tuesday, March 7, 2000: Well, interesting developments occurred today. I had a great conversation with Nathan Johnston, thanking him again for cautioning me on Sunday that, although I was having a peaceful day, the anger would surface again soon, and that sure enough, yesterday, it had.

When it did, I told him, I was okay with it, remembering what he had said. I wanted to see if Reverend Johnston had any more words of advice. I also wanted his opinion on the wisdom of looking for a new job at this juncture. He gave me an excellent analogy. He pointed out that when one is in a car wreck and one's body is broken up, it takes time to heal, and one allows oneself time to heal.

What has happened to me is also a breaking up, but it is internal. He said I have lost something — my innocence — and that I will go through stages of grief over that loss. He said to be very kind to myself, don't forget to breathe, and allow myself to feel. He said the problem comes when one gets stuck in, for example, grief, or perhaps sadness or depression. It's okay to feel all these things, but not to allow oneself to get stuck.

Well, I also went to see my therapist, and we talked about many interesting things there! She talked about "taking it to a higher level" with people. When I spoke of my love-making experiences of late (since I remembered my past), she asked, "What is the BEST that it can be?"

For me, right now, the best is absolutely when I am pretending to be a French woman and allowing myself to totally get into it and totally enjoy it and immerse myself in the experience.

She said that that is not only the best way, it is the way that it is meant to be, a good and holy and Godly experience of mind, body, and soul. She said that making love is truly an exchange of energy, to enjoy the maleness and the femaleness.

I left there today feeling very much at peace and feeling like anything is possible, including healing. She also said to more or less identify with my stepdaughter, Katy, when she is connecting with her dad. I can try to enjoy the experience of their connection and allow my heart to follow. Rather than getting stuck in the jealousy mode, I can take it to the higher level. I am trying that tonight. I can become a part of it!

Thursday, April 20, 2000: I have been remiss, not writing in so long. Last week, on Sunday I believe (April 16th) I was having trouble going to sleep. Tomas had already fallen asleep and so I decided to try using the *"Ommmmmm"* chant to get to sleep.

As I quietly repeated the sound, I became more and more relaxed and then, I started hearing footsteps.

I KNEW they weren't real footsteps, but I decided to "go with it." (I see now that at times, feeling extremely safe with Tomas next to me, that this is when I am best able to unearth old memories.) So, I was hearing footsteps, slowly and deliberately coming up the steps (only there are no such steps here so I knew I was safe and only in a self-hypnotic state).

Then, I realized it was HIM, coming up the steps at my childhood home on Maple Street, slowly but surely, and I was in my bed, under my covers, totally helpless and unprotected and absolutely terrified, knowing that hiding under my covers in the night would not protect me from this monster, my father.

I remember listening to him climb those steps, and I do remember feeling incredibly relieved when he would crawl into one of the other beds, with one of my other sisters.

I did not wake Tomas up but fell asleep and the next morning, I shared my story with my good friend, Laura, at my old job where I remain employed for now. I am SO GLAD I did, as she was able to help me see a much bigger picture than I had heretofore.

When I told her how much shock I have been in, she said, "As well you should!" She said if I was NOT in shock, something would be seriously wrong and she cautioned me that, although I want to bypass all the suffering and reliving and experiencing the rough feelings and skip right to the healing and forgiving phase, that it won't and can't happen that way. She cautioned me to be kind to myself, and she cried with me and we hugged. I feel blessed that I have her as a friend.

Easter Sunday, April 23, 2000. We had Mother and Dad to dinner tonight, along with Aunt Jenny and Aunt Beth. It was not a happy meal for me but at least all went smoothly. I am hoping Mother will go to Maribeth Hart's with me for my therapy session on Tuesday, although I must confess, I am very much in touch with my anger at this point.

December of 2001: An amazing thing happened today!!! I was driving in my car and approaching a stop sign. Suddenly, an immense owl with its wings outstretched flew right in front of my windshield, straighter than an arrow and with unbelievable speed!!

If I had maintained my rate of speed rather than decelerating as I approached the stop sign, the owl would have collided with my windshield with incredible force. I slowed down a little more as I watched, astounded, as the owl brushed by my car, whizzing by more closely to me than anything in nature normally would.

Wow! I thought. *What was that? Why was that owl headed straight FOR me?!? A fluke? A sign? A message from somewhere, or from Someone?*

If a message it was meant to be, then what?

Why an owl? Why me? Owls equate with wisdom. This one was majestic, powerful, and straight on a course. When I saw it, I was on my way to a final exam for one of my college courses, ill with vertigo and a urinary tract infection and feeling anything but wise and confident.

Could it have really been a message, intended for stupid, insignificant me?

That thought not only touched me, it humbled me and moved me to tears. Then, the tears flowed, which was actually just what I needed.

For more than twenty years, I put my heart and soul into loving, raising, teaching, and nurturing two sons. How I miss the boys that they were! How I miss their hugs and their smiles, their laughter, and their love!

For, despite all my best efforts, I "lost" one, the younger, to drugs (he now resides with my ex-husband). The other one, the older, I've lost to the bitterness of my ex-husband it seems, or perhaps to his own bitterness and pain from losing his father at age nine. The older, I suspect, blames me for his dad falling out of his life. He at one point said he believes it was manipulation by me that kept his natural father out of his life for ten years, when in reality I fled that marriage, due to Peter's cocaine addiction and my (very healthy) fear that we would both end up in jail, leaving no one to raise our sons.

But the pain of having his father totally out of his life for ten years must be so great that he has to blame someone. The irony is that, in shouldering the cloak of bitterness that his birth dad also wears, my older son does not now see that he is being manipulated in the opposite direction — shutting me out of his life.

In this unbelievably crazy world, I have once again been assigned my childhood role of "scapegoat." This time by my son! How convenient it is to blame everything on the mother.

My younger son was homeless for years and now lives with my ex-husband. He was recently (finally) seen by a therapist and diagnosed with severe depression exacerbated by substance abuse. He stayed on medication for only a short while and seems to be so negative and sad still, and everything I have tried has seemed to make things worse for him. So, I stay away, and pray.

There is not a day that goes by that I do not miss my sons and wish it could be and could have been otherwise for them. It is a constant, painful, open wound that indeed is so awful that it has driven me once again back to school, in a healthy direction of escape.

I miss them — terribly. Oh, the younger one calls, once in a blue moon. But the older, he has completely discarded his stepfather (Tomas) and me and his stepsister like old, used up, unwanted rags. He has no time for us. There's not even a monthly phone call or a ten-minute visit on his birthday or on a holiday!! How incredible!! That what was once such a loving, sensitive, caring, responsible son could so totally and utterly turn and reject those who loved and nurtured him, laughed with him and grew with him for twenty-one and a half years is beyond heart-breaking!

Thus, thanks to the owl, I released some of my anguish. I cried and felt better for it. Thank you, dear owl, for those tears, and for intervening.

I do know that the little boys I sorely miss can only be visited in my dreams. They are men now and things have become so much more complicated for them, for me, and for us.

I need to straighten out my own thoughts, my own emotions, my own story, if you will, and then, hopefully, there will be room in all our lives for true healing and at least some sort of connection with each other.

January 4, 2002: Today is Ben's second birthday! I cannot believe it has been TWO years since I went down to Florida and almost two years since I remembered!!! I am only now beginning to write my entire story thus far, realizing that if I do not continue to document it, when I am gone, it too will be gone.

I've been dying to write down a recent lucid dream. Only of late have I begun having them again. I love it when, in a dream, I realize that I AM dreaming and thus, become "awake and aware" within the dream and able to do anything imaginable.

I awoke in my dream and decided to get out of my body. I got way out, into the stars of the universe where all is black except for the stars and it was here that I had a unique experience. As I was getting out, I experienced MYSELF as pure energy, electrified and sparking and really, just like electricity, very strong.

It was neither pleasant nor unpleasant. It just WAS! I was pure energy, that's all. No fear, no emotion, no surprise, just the energy of being. Then, I became startled to see, against the background of blackness of outer space, my own reflection. It was like whiteness on a photography negative, sort of, but not exactly.

What I saw was a series of reflections, of all the faces I have worn, have been in this life, from little girl forward, and it occurred to me just how many faces I have had. After seeing so many faces, it seemed as though the experience would either turn positive or negative for me at this point. I did not trust that this was leading me to a place I wanted to go. Perhaps I did not want to see my present face or to be allowed to see future faces. I am not sure what made me hesitate, but I ended it and woke up. Upon waking, I felt empowered and invigorated by this amazing awareness of existing as a sparkling being of energy.

I would define it as energy in directed form. That is what we are. Period. Energy. We can choose to be helpful or harmful, positive or negative, to use that energy in this way or that. But it is not inherently either one.

Once we realize that it absolutely is a choice, the choice becomes pretty simple. The trick is to keep your eye on the source, that is, at the very least, to maintain an awareness of what we human beings actually are — pure energy.

Energy that is neither good nor bad. Energy that is wearing a cloak of warm, soft, beautiful, living, breathing flesh. Religions that deem us "evil" or "sinful" from the start are unfortunate and not at all helpful or healthy, in my opinion.

Our bodies, like our energy, are neither good nor bad. They are life begetting life. Like a burning candle, they just are. Our bodies are the wax. Our heart is the wick. Our energy is the flame. That's the way it is. The wax will not sustain the wick and the flame forever, but here is where the candle analogy must end.

Our energy, unlike a flame, but exactly as Albert Einstein miraculously realized, can neither be created nor destroyed. It just is, and it will continue to be.

What struck me the most profoundly in this experiencing of my energy or rather of myself AS pure energy and just energy . . . is that this energy was and is neither good nor bad. We just are. These ideas of good and bad are value judgments which, in ways, have inflicted such utter damage on our experience of who we truly are that they in and of themselves are often not helpful. They harm because they do tend to falsely color our experience.

They limit and thus imprison our thoughts and our perceptions. They can enshroud us in fear, cloud our perceptions, and mislead us in unhealthy ways. There's one other crucial thing worth noting. This experience, this actual sensing of myself as burning, flickering, pulsating, crackling energy — it was not in the least bit scary. On the contrary, it was simply pure aliveness, neither pleasant nor unpleasant. It was one experience which I know I shall never be able to do justice to in words because there is no frame of reference for it and no words which can precisely suit it.

No prior experience compares. Pleasure, discomfort, fear, joy, and pain were all in a sense revealed to be irrelevant and unimportant. The evil inflicted upon my childhood self injured me deeply, but, after dealing with the overwhelming anger, I can choose to rise above it all and seek a positive path.

There was such a strength in the crackling energy, a sense of utter stability in the midst of complete movement, a permanence and not exactly peace but something closer to a security that comes from stability.

I know now with a 110% certainty that yes, these particular bodies will pass out of existence eventually, but it doesn't matter because the energy within, the true being, will not and indeed cannot "die."

It will be transformed, will obviously take SOMETHING out of the experience here on earth with it, but will absolutely be transformed or perhaps once again simply be REVEALED and will continue . . . on and on.

There truly is no hard and fast "reality." There is only, in this here and now, and absolutely only, one's perception of it, limited by the beliefs we choose to believe, by the thoughts and actions we choose to focus on, and by our choices. And the less "tainted" or "colored" or "confined" that we allow those perceptions to be, the BROADER we become, and the broader our experiences become, the deeper and fuller, and more meaningful our very existence is, and I suspect, the greater is our potential to manifest, to create, to grow, and to love.

This experience has left a happy and hopeful feeling in me that is sustaining me through the dark coldness of winter's days.

February 15, 2002: I cannot believe it has been two years ago today that I remembered about the violent kiss, the first of several "rememberings." To this day, Jenna does not know, nor does she want to know what I remembered, which seems so strange to me. I did tell Jackie and Karen about the "high man" eventually, despite the fact that Jackie refused to try to remember it herself, which I can now understand. She did protect me from him to a degree, but no one protected her.

To this day, I sometimes feel the anger. A few days ago, I went to kiss Tomas and for no reason, wanted to kiss him roughly, angrily. And I thought, *What is this?*

That's how I remembered – the two-year anniversary was approaching. So, this morning, I got up, put my schoolwork and housework aside, and sat at this computer for hours, writing, editing my story, searching for a "closure" of some sorts. It will, of course, never be closed. And my story, also, has not yet ended. I am, in two weeks, headed down to Jacksonville to spend time with Jackie who now lives there with her second husband. I really haven't spent any length of time with my sister since she married her first husband in the 1970s.

One thing is for sure — it hasn't been a boring life!

I never wrote about it until now, but I did take Mother to my therapist's office, and it was an interesting session. Mother cried when I recounted how she tried to protect Jenna, tried to keep my father from hurting her. I do think that Carl Stephens was extremely sick and that our mother was utterly terrified of him, and so accepted a position of powerlessness for many years. Thankfully, at long last, she divorced him. It took her fifteen long years to break free of him. By that time, I was eleven years old.

I also forgot to journal that when I spoke to my therapist about my fears around my own loss of virginity, she said that it doesn't matter if I remember more or not. She said that the already remembered incest was enough and that I was not to worry about remembering more.

Sometimes, I think I should major in psychology. Sometimes, I think I should go into medicine. For now, my educational path at the university is computer science, and I am very grateful to be back in school with only one year remaining until I attain my degree. Amazing!

February 9, 2003: How incredible it is to me that it has been almost three years since the memory of the worst abuse resurfaced in my mind. If not for a wonderful friend (June), there might not be much more to document, but I am, after all, writing this, thanks to her, and thanks to the turtle.

Last September, in the beginning of my senior year at college, a classmate announced that she and her husband were going to the beach for a week of vacation. Since this was at the beginning of the semester, I offered to tape the lectures from the classes that we shared, to help keep her work current in those classes. She gratefully accepted my offer. During the week she was absent, I audiotaped the classes for her, as I had promised. That way, upon her return, she could catch up on what she had missed.

At that time, this particular classmate was little more than an acquaintance. Even though she was not a close friend of mine, I had shared with her a little of what was happening in my life: that I was attending Penn State University in part for the ulterior motive of trying not to focus on my empty nest and on how much I missed my two sons. I also told her that I had recently remembered things about my childhood but did not go into detail. (It took, in the end, almost a year of friendship before I trusted her with that whole story.)

When June returned from the beach, she called me and told me that I was "not going to believe" what had happened to her while on vacation. When I asked her what had happened, she refused to tell me over the phone, insisting that I wait until Monday, when she would see me, to hear the story face to face. She piqued my curiosity even more when she stated that the unbelievable occurrence, whatever it was, involved me "in a big way." She stated that she wouldn't tell me because she feared that I would think she was crazy.

On Monday, we ran into each other outside, on the walkway leading to the library.

After waiting all weekend to hear her story, I immediately asked, "Hi, June! Please tell me now, what happened at the beach?"

"I can't tell you," she insisted. "I forgot to bring the object with me to school, and it's crucial to the story."

"Please, please, you must tell me!" I implored.

"Well, alright," she relented. "My significant other, Sam, our infant son, and my mother had a really great week at Ocean City, Maryland. On the way back home, we found that we had some extra time and because we had never been there before, decided to stop and visit Atlantic City, New Jersey, for a few hours. Well, my mom was in the casino and Sam was watching the baby. I wanted to walk down the boardwalk along the beach, and so I did. To my surprise, an old woman called out to me as I walked by."

June continued her story, a tale she thought I'd never believe.

"Do you know Susie?" the old woman had asked.

"What?" my friend had replied, as she tried to keep walking.

"Susie?" the old woman persisted. "You have a friend named Susie, don't you? And she has many problems?"

The old woman spoke broken English. She was sitting on a stool, with a box of paints by her side. She had few teeth and spoke in an accent. She had dark hair and, according to June, looked like a "gypsy" woman.

Confused and startled, my friend replied: "Well, yes, I do, but—"

"Tell me about Susie's problems," the old woman directed. She pulled out a little figurine and began to paint colors on it. "You talk," she said. "I paint."

At this point in the tale, my friend stopped, glancing at me to see if I might be angry that she had shared what she knew of my personal problems with this total stranger. Mesmerized, I was not. I urged her to continue.

The gypsy lady with the dark hair sat on her stool and pulled from her box a tiny figurine, a turtle. She began painting, as my friend told her about me and my problems. And then, June stopped.

"No, more!" the gypsy woman protested. "You talk; I paint."

And so, my friend told her all that she knew, down to the last detail, until there was no more to tell. When she was done, the woman handed her the figurine and said:

"Give this to Susie. Tell her it will bring her luck."

My friend took the turtle and asked the woman what she owed her, but the woman refused payment, even when June insisted on paying her something. The woman simply stated:

"Susie will pay me back some day. I will see her, some day."

The minute June handed me the turtle, I loved it immensely. Little did I realize that it was another piece of the puzzle, a link to my long-lost childhood memories, the link that would fill in what I hope are the last missing pieces of the puzzle. I did not think June crazy due to her experience, and she, in turn, accepted me despite my oddities.

All I knew at that point was that, for the first time in my long life of truly believing in the existence of real "magic" in the universe, I finally had proof positive that "magical" experiences (unseen, unexplainable phenomena) absolutely do occur.

June truly feared that I would think that she was totally crazy. Little did she know me then. I knew that June was not a drinker, not a drug addict, and not a psychotic, and that the tale must be true, down to the last detail.

In my deepest soul, I triumphantly cried, *YES!* And I fell totally in love with that amazing, hand-painted turtle. Of course, I was also still curious as to how I was to repay the old woman. The tantalizing fact that the adventure was not yet complete loomed before me as I hugged June, my most special friend.

I took the turtle home and showed it to my husband. He was standing at our back door, looking out the window, and I placed the tiny turtle in the palm of his hand. An amazing thing happened. The instant he held it in his open hand and was glancing down upon it, I saw, with a jolt and a shock, not my husband, but my birth father standing there before me, holding a turtle!!! Tomas, for that instant, completely and utterly turned into my father. I had what I now know was a flashback.

What is this?! I wondered. I remembered that we had turtles as pets, and they were not much fun because they did not move around much in their turtle bowl and often stunk.

Their plastic bowl had a walkway, coming up out of the water, but it was usually not kept very clean, and it was smelly. Usually, when we were allowed to buy turtles, they would end up dead.

So, why, I wondered, *would I remember my father, holding a turtle in his hand? What did that mean? What had happened?*

The answer to that mystery was not immediately forthcoming.

There was a second flashback that occurred with that turtle as well. This gift from a gypsy lady at the beach, sent through my classmate, was connecting me to my past — past memories I had forgotten. The chilling fact is that no other object besides a turtle could have elicited such a response from me.

That first flashback occurred soon after June gave me the turtle, but it was not until more than one month later, on November 21, 2002, that I experienced the second, more shocking flashback.

That day in late November, Tomas and I were beginning to make love, caressing each other with intimate gentleness. Tomas' touch brushed in an intimate place and for one horrifying instant, again for just the briefest of moments, he completely turned into my father, my father with an evil smile on his face.

This flashback smacked me like a million volts of electricity. I shall never forget the look on his face (my father's) in that instant, and the terror that surged through me upon seeing, instead of Tomas, my father's horrific, threatening expression. It was such a shock that, at the time, I could not even mention it to my husband.

Seriously, just exactly how DOES one say, in the beginning stages of lovemaking, "Oh, by the way, you just turned into *mia padre* for an instant . . . and no, but thanks for asking, I'm really not going off the deep end . . . "?!!?

YUK! I couldn't believe it. The place that Tomas had gently touched me was, of all places, the rearmost! In that brief moment, I totally and most undeniably saw my father there, next to me, with an evil smile.

Though that flashback was akin to lightning striking yet again, there is no doubt in my mind that that was, quite simply, some type of flashback or resurfacing of a long-buried memory that exploded out of my mind like a mini volcanic eruption.

Through subsequent hypnotherapy, the memories more fully resurfaced. Yes, I was raped, but not in the typical fashion, if indeed one can say that there ever is a "typical" fashion of rape.

It has been so traumatic that I was unable to write about it as I went through this remembering process, similar to the experience of remembering what happened to my baby sister on the changing table. Through the Grace of God, I retain enough sanity to recount it now.

As a persistent and determined four-year-old, I had pushed and pushed and pushed the "high man" question until the monster known as my father felt (I suppose) that he had no other choice. He decided to take drastic action.

※

I recall his gentleness as he lifted me into his lap and lovingly began to caress me. I enjoyed his loving touch. I was, like all innocent children, open and welcoming to love and affection from either parent. Adults often tickle or pat little ones in sensitive places, and my father at first gently caressed my tiny butt. It was an abrupt shift from that fatherly affection and caress to unexpected pain that brutally shook my world in a way neither before nor since experienced.

One second, I was being held by him on his lap, the loving daughter being affectionately cuddled and loved, and in the next instant, I was brutally violated in the innermost region, one without a tell-tale hymen, with a rough, hard and unforgiving finger whose sole intent was to inflict pain, to violate, oppress and stifle, to conquer, to terrorize, and in the end, to rape and win silence. As I squirmed and tried to break free, he tightened his steely grip with his free hand and pulled me closer to him and to that sickening smell of beer, closer to his dripping fear and desperation, his free hand also stifling my screams.

"This is what a high man is!" he growled *"It is that part of you that I can go high into, like this!"*

He made sure that he was as "high" as he could be, twisting and hurting me as much as he possibly could.

"You had to know! You wouldn't give it up, so now, you do know. This is a high man. Now, do you understand?!" he cruelly declared.

His brutishness had sufficiently tortured me. He waited until my cries revealed defeat before releasing me, and letting me go, I crumpled and curled into a whimpering ball.

The worst part about it was that no one knew what had happened, and no one comforted or consoled me or tended to my wounds, both physical and psychological. It would eventually become a forgotten event that my conscious mind blotted out, as sometimes happens with trauma. However, the most intimate cells in my body recalled it with a stark vividness and my relationship with my body and its most intimate functions was forever changed.

※

Shortly after that, my unstoppable mind bombarded me with questions. Even at my young age, none of it made sense. Why had I been so severely hurt for asking what seemed to be a very important question? How could there be a high "man" within a girl? How could it be in two places on me, but in only one place on Jenna? And why did it hurt so much? Did it hurt for everyone? What really was a high man? Why was my father lying? Why was it so important?

And so, once again, I dared to inquire once more, very secretively, very quietly, but somehow, he knew that I had. At the time, he said nothing. But a few days later, he and I were once again alone in the house. We were in the living room, and he walked over to our pet turtles' bowl and picked up one little turtle. He looked down at me, glaring into my eyes and spoke as I looked at the turtle sitting in his out-stretched hand.

"If I ever hear you asking even one more person about the high man, I will take this turtle and put it as high in you with my finger as before, and I will leave it there. It will eat you alive, from the inside out! Then, you WILL stop asking!"

I now knew that he meant business, and I had no doubt that he would do exactly what he had said. The sheer horror of that thought resulted in my long-coveted silence. I froze, terrified once again, and waiting for this horrible encounter to end, fearful that Father would set the turtle loose in me then and there, and that it would horribly, slowly, eat me alive from the inside out!!

"Do you understand?" he asked.

Too afraid to open my mouth and speak, I nodded, beaten down and defeated at last. Despite my terror, my two tiny legs somehow maintained me on two feet as I stood my ground, expecting the worst. It was a tremendous relief to watch Father bend over and return the turtle to its bowl and to hear his tone soften somewhat as he said I could now go to my room. I exhaled and quickly ran to my room.

I now knew that no adult, the only ones who truly knew all the answers, would ever tell me what I desperately needed to know. I knew that if I continued to ask, my father would indeed take the turtle and do as he had said. And so it was that I finally stopped asking the high man question.

Unanswered, it became buried in the deepest recesses of my mind. At the time, I told no one what had happened nor was my mind able to logically process and store the memories of those traumatic events because so much of it made no sense at all and simply "did not compute."

As sometimes happens with trauma and shock, my mind went on to other things, leaving the crucial questions unanswered. Those bad memories were suppressed, buried for decades until, within the safety of a warm, loving relationship, they slowly, amazingly resurfaced.

Although my father, in a sense, won the struggle when I was little, in that he did indeed at that time silence me, he did not, in the final analysis, win. In remembering, in writing about my childhood, in sharing all these events, I actually won and continue to win!

My father was a tormented and demented soul, who did nothing more and nothing less than pass on a family legacy of incest, to not only my two older sisters, but to baby Jenna and me as well, never realizing that he was being influenced and controlled by the energies and edicts of generations past, something that I've worked hard not to pass on to my children.

After these painful memories were recalled, I went through quite a period of re-adjusting to my own body and to my sexuality. Actually, my sexuality was basically put "on hold" for quite some time.

I now detested the feeling of nature's bodily eliminations. This lasted for weeks, and for what seemed like months, I had a rough time with daily functions. Truly and in fact, throughout my life, I had had trouble in that arena, and now, at long last, I knew why!

I have never had a good relationship with either of my elimination processes, and now, finally, at the age of forty-nine, I learn why. I wet the bed as a child. I even had a bowel resection several years ago, having suffered a bowel obstruction immediately following a partial hysterectomy. One can only wonder now if that childhood trauma had perhaps at least partially contributed to the cause of those ailments.

Words fall short of conveying the impact of something so intimately personal and so basic and primal. For as long as I can remember, I have had difficulties. Perhaps, now that I know why, this relationship with my body might change. This is most difficult to delicately document, to continue to think about in an attempt to face it, and most importantly, to heal and somehow come to peace with it.

A few weeks ago, I felt I had at long last, made at least temporary peace with my systems. One day at work, after working particularly hard at the office, I rewarded myself with a relaxing break in the ladies' room. That ladies' room has a wonderfully comfortable and private stall with a built-in heater under the window, and a ledge containing magazines for reading. It has a homey feeling, and I had just received a compliment, a very rare occurrence from my boss. I felt good, and I felt satisfied.

I went in and just relaxed in there, alone and at peace and feeling satisfaction from my own accomplishments and feeling entitled to a break. I relaxed and just enjoyed the process. Since then, I have from time to time actually been able to enjoy nature's workings.

It was, as stated above, well after receiving the turtle from June, at the end of September 2002, that I remembered all of this — in late November. And it was only about a week ago (the beginning of February) that I felt something reawaken in me and began to feel the desire for my husband again. I feel so fortunate to be healing at all.

I do hesitate to share any of this with my sisters and/or my mother and adopted dad now, especially since I do believe Karen was similarly violated, although I do believe and hope not quite so violently and deeply as I was. Therefore, I shall for now remain silent.

Thank you, June, for being such a good friend and for bringing me the last piece of the puzzle. Or, perhaps, is this just the latest piece of the puzzle? I had once believed that I had "remembered it all" and then, more resurfaced.

I am very fortunate that I am studying psychology and am thus able to maintain some objectivity and try to make some sense of all of this. At least, I feel I have written down my story to date.

I know I am also very lucky to have such an understanding and tolerant husband.

March 8, 2003: Strange how a little knowledge can be a "dangerous thing" or sometimes, I guess, an awfully confusing one. I think I have depths and depths of anger in me, and now, when I am angry at this or at that, I find myself wondering, *is this "displaced anger"?*

I ask myself, *am I so angry because deep down inside, the one I am really angry at, primarily angry with, is my father? Or is it my mother?*

The definition of *displacement* is more or less that it is the defense mechanism that occurs when an individual shifts unacceptable feelings from one object to another more acceptable object. The definition of *displaced anger* is when we feel anger at one person (for example, a boss) and take it out on someone more acceptable or safer (for example, a spouse).

Perhaps it is not so much displacement of my anger as it is that I have such an abundance of repressed rage that, when I do allow myself to feel anger at all, it is, in essence, an overabundance of anger that erupts. Perhaps it is not so much displaced as merely suppressed anger, or perhaps it's both.

This morning, I found I was feeling sorry for myself and wondering if I will ever be able to experience a morning constitution without thinking of what my father did to me. Actually, in just thinking about writing that, I realize the stages that I have already come through. In rereading this diary, I realize that there are times when I don't even think of him and when I have been able to relax and enjoy it.

Actually, part of what is on my mind this morning is that I want to replay the recent audiotaped hypnotherapy session (during which I recalled the rape). I guess I am afraid that doing so will make me terribly depressed or at the very least freaked out. Yet, it seems like something that must be done. There must be a way to "process" this, to fully and finally put it to rest and move beyond it.

I have so much to do: current homework, study for the psych GRE (the Graduate Record Examination, a standardized test used for admission to graduate schools), study for the regular GRE, figure out what I am doing as to the French trip that I am taking in April with a Penn State University group, and normal housework. My to-do list also includes working out at the gym, taking care of myself (massage, meditation), practicing my singing lessons, finishing sewing the pants I hope to take to France, and of course, working on this diary.

It is a beautiful, sunny day today, but I do not feel happy, even though we might ride our bicycles this afternoon.

March 11, 2003: Today, I finally did it! It was a sunny, peaceful day and I braved listening to the tape recording of the November 21, 2002, hypnotherapy session wherein I recalled the rape. I actually listened to it en route to and from the endodontist. I had a root canal check appointment. The tape was very sad but overall, it is almost inaudible. Much of what I said I cannot hear, although of course the feelings, the pain, the fear, and the grief all come across very clearly. There were, in addition to the rape, a couple of interesting remembrances that came out during the session.

"Pushing the envelope." Mother and Father often used to chastise me for pushing the envelope when it came to things, meaning I took things too far and got myself into trouble (as I had "pushed" the question of the high man). It was a favorite phrase of theirs and was always spoken in a harsh tone, placing full responsibility for the outcome(s) on my misbehavior.

"For good measure" was also a phrase that Mother liked to use when talking about punishment. I can almost hear her saying it now, as harshly and vehemently as she did then when she doled out punishment for this or for that.

"And, for good measure, you will not get dessert

tonight!" she would declare, associating the word good with something that was not the least bit good at all.

Truly, I am so relieved that, after almost four months, I found the courage to listen to this tape. It was, you see, the one thing I was truly afraid of. I think that in this life, we move forward the best and grow the most by doing or at least attempting to do, those things that we ARE most afraid of. After listening to the tape, I feel stronger and somehow closer to some closure about these horrors that I have uncovered.

I told Tomas I had listened to the tape and he had nothing to say. I think my poor baby wants to forget about all of this, in part so that he will not find himself hating my mother.

Sunday, March 16, 2003: Wow! I called my step-daughter, Katy, today in England for the first time. Tomas had trouble getting through on the numbers she had given and when I tried, an operator came on the line and assisted. So, I was happy to get through and to at last hear her voice.

On her end, I heard a male voice in her room, and she explained to him, "It's my Mom" in a happy voice.

Man, my heart sure soared to hear her refer to me, her stepmother, as her Mom!! We had a lovely conversation, ending with me giving her instructions about her student loan and handing the phone to Tomas. I had called and done research here in the States for her this week to ascertain how she could defer her student loan. She had been unable to figure it out on her own.

After we got off the phone, I did share with Tomas that she had referred to me as "Mom" and I think it made him extremely happy, too. For the rest of the day, he treated me with such exquisite tenderness and adoring love, such as I had not experienced in quite some time. Perhaps, hopefully, we will actually be able to move beyond the hurdles we have been stuck in for so long, as to all three of our children. That includes mine as well. I wonder if either of my sons will ever refer to their stepfather as their dad. I hope that'll happen.

I feel that it is truly my success that Katy did think of me and referred to me as her "mom," and I pat myself on the back. It is, at long last, a tangible testimony to the myriad of positive and loving, motherly words and actions that I have endeavored to bestow upon her, despite her difficult jealousy of me and sometimes spoiled behavior. This was in spite of her best attempts to paint me as the "evil stepmother" in the eyes of her father, to sway him her way to get her own way.

It is my hope that I can somehow "set an example" that will eventually result in lasting peace throughout our now extended step family. That is, of course, my goal in addition to my primary goal of helping others wherever, whenever, and however possible, whether or not deserved, desired, or reciprocated. I have, with Katy, often turned the other cheek and now I see why this is the wisest position to take in life, anywhere, at any time and with anyone.

Tuesday, March 18, 2003: Well, it's a beautiful day and a beautiful week, spring having finally sprung! We had a wonderful weekend bike ride with Karen and Rick. And I rode with June yesterday, too.

I feel totally spoiled this week, as I am not working due to the vacation of one of the attorneys and there is no work for me at the office. At home, I have a gazillion things to do. I am looking forward to graduation, the French trip, our first summer without any of our kids living under our roof, hummingbirds in our yard (and perhaps the neighbor children's yard as well), bicycling with friends, exploring new places, finding a new job (hopefully, a more satisfying one), the pancake weekend with Karen and Rick, seeing the new Omnimax movie, and so much more. Life feels like a wonderful adventure, and I thank God that we have at least a shot at enjoying this summer to the max, hopefully basking in the glow of graduation, love, and loved ones.

Sunday, March 30, 2003: Well, shortly after midnight "today" — I had an interesting "breakthrough." There are lovemaking sessions which are memorable for one reason or another and this was undoubtedly one of them. It was different in that I both abandoned myself and yet at the same time was able to connect more with myself than ever before. The only thought in my head was "pure pleasure" — I was experiencing the pleasure as both pure in a total sense and pure in a clean, white sense. I became aware of only myself.

As my awareness of the universe faded, I fully sensed my own strong yet deliciously intense pleasure, my loud and rapid breathing, and my hot and increasingly aroused body. I had one fleeting thought: *If my lover had made but one little noise, it would have "broken" the moment.*

Fortunately, I have THE best husband and that did not happen. He was silent and as usual, perfect in lovemaking. I was experiencing exquisitely extreme pleasure but somehow unable to fully let go when something happened to again confirm my absolute conviction that unseen hands, unbeknownst to us, constantly orchestrate our lives.

Years ago, a loud, annoying fire siren was installed in our neighborhood. This was several years after we had purchased our home. It rings day or night, often sounding for several minutes at a time, sometimes triggering a headache in me. It is THAT loud. Fortunately, sometimes for weeks, we will not hear the fire alarm at all. Then, shattering the silence, it rings. Today, for one blissful instance, it was anything but an annoyance.

As I was suspended in total arousal and at just that instant when a hint of fear at the prospect of totally letting go began to dawn, unbidden, into my psyche, a sound pierced the night, at precisely the right instant, helping me reach just a little further, a little higher, a little beyond where I had dared reach — that fire siren rang loud and clear at just the right moment!

This typically annoying siren became a wild and freeing trumpet, its ringing but a screaming howling at the moon. The blaring heightened the intensity and wildness of the moment and invited me to fully let go. I braved total abandonment, so intense and complete that I partially blacked out.

Afterward, I felt like shouting, *YES!*

This stands as a super "sweet revenge" against the hurts of the past, and those who hurt me. It is, I believe, not only pleasure but more importantly, a triumph, a success, a moving towards an increasingly healthy emotional, spiritual and physical state, but, of course, a team effort it was. I can show my appreciation to my lover, my husband, but how do I thank those unseen hands, those spirits? Only a blind fool would think that, for the siren to have sounded at that exact and precise moment in time, it was but mere coincidence.

The way I see it, the odds of that siren going off at just that precise exact moment of pending orgasm are quite small indeed.

Friday, April 4, 2003: Last night, I had the greatest dream. I had been sleeping without my mouth guard for a few nights now, hoping that I will not have the angry dreams about my son, Jack (during which I grind my teeth), which necessitated my use of the mouth guard in the first place. About eight or nine months ago, I ended up with two root canals from grinding my teeth due to an angry dream about Jack's total absence from our lives.

Recently, I made it a goal to get over that anger and thus, be able to sleep without the mouth guard so that I don't have to take it to France. A few nights ago, I did dream of him wherein he was with us but his wife, Deborah, was not. He was okay though he was angry on some levels with Deborah, actually. It was an odd dream, but the important thing for me was that I was not angry with him in that dream. I would like to free myself from the anger and from the need for this mouth guard before my trip to France.

In last night's dream, I found myself listening to a middle-aged woman, a mother, talking to someone else about her children. She was upset that they were not visiting her enough. She said that it's bad enough that they have to leave, but once they do leave home, they should come home to visit at least every weekend. She genuinely believed that she was right, that is, that her children owed her that much, to at least call or visit each and every weekend.

"You're wrong!" I told her. "You have to realize that your children are busy building their own lives and to put a restriction or expectation on them like that could only be destructive to both ends of the relationship. You would be lucky if they contacted you once a month. Once a month is healthy."

I started to tell her, sadly but not angrily, the situation with my sons, and then, I woke up.

I am hoping that this means that, on a subconscious level as well, that I realize that when my sons do not call or give me much of their time, it is not due to any lack of love on their part but rather due to the busy and demanding nature of their lives. I also realize that one should be grateful that they are standing independently on their own two feet, and although struggling, are still out in the world and hopefully enjoying loving relationships with the partners that they have freely chosen.

It is one of the most extremely difficult things to do, to really let go of one's kids, but I think I have done it, and I think it is healthy and that I can be at peace in this regard.

Sunday, April 6, 2003: After the last lovemaking session, every time that fire alarm goes off in the neighborhood, instead of being annoyed, I find myself aroused. Although sometimes we do not hear it for weeks, this "Pavlov's dog" reaction occurs when the siren blares.

The downside of an excellent experience like that is that it is hard if not impossible to top it the next time. Yet, today I enjoyed an equally memorable lovemaking experience. I should mention that, of late, intercourse has been somewhat physically painful. It only recently occurred to me while meditating that perhaps this is not physical, since it is a recent change that occurred since remembering the rape. I did mention this to my therapist, but she did not respond. This indicated in my mind that perhaps I am on point, and that she possibly has no solution.

Nonetheless, there is, thankfully more than one way to skin the cat and, as noted above, I am blessed with the most loving, free, tolerant, patient, and gently unselfish lover who affords me great freedom of expression, if you will. This time, though decidedly different from the last, was just as memorable. I did not lose consciousness, and it was not quite as intense. Neither did the neighborhood siren enhance my success.

Yet, when I climaxed, I just freely and deliciously came and came and came and came . . .

Monday, April 7, 2003: Today, I am filled with such love for others that I sent off two loving cards, one to my daughter-in-law to be, Lynn, telling her how much I appreciate the love and happiness that she has brought into Lee's life, and the other to my daughter-in-law, Deborah, telling her the following:

"I don't believe I have ever made known to you the depth of the gratitude in my heart for the joy you have brought into my son's life. Thank you for putting the biggest smile on his face that I have ever seen. The important thing to me, always, is that he is happy and healthy and moving in a positive direction! Thank you."

Tuesday, April 15, 2003: Lee said that Lynn really loved the card that I sent. I did not hear from Jack and Deborah. I hope that they did receive the card and that it was accepted in the spirit in which it was intended.

Wednesday, April 23, 2003: As part of graduation from the music/voice class I'm completing at the university, I was required to perform, to sing three songs in public, which I did today. It is difficult to express how wonderfully this mandatory guitar playing and public singing recital on the university campus lawn went today.

Because the weather was so chilly, there were fortunately only a handful of students outside for my first "performance." That was utterly perfect for me since, even with so few in my audience, I was extremely nervous. I got through it fine though I know it was not my best performance of the three songs I ended up playing and singing. Yes, I actually did THREE sets of the three songs in total, as my professor had instructed!

After the first set, I went back inside the main building, as my wonderful voice teacher had suggested, had a drink, and talked a little with some friends. Then, I went back outside. The second performance was MUCH stronger. After the second song, a fellow student remarked, "You're really sounding good!" I enjoyed singing the second set more and was able to just get into the singing and playing more, and found I was losing myself in it and becoming less self-conscious.

I had planned on meeting Elizabeth, the friend with whom I will soon be spending a month in France, God willing. She arrived late, and I decided to play that third set just for her. I had seen her perform her Irish dancing (the River Dance type of dance) last semester. She was very good. I thought that, in turn, it would be well if she saw that I, too, have some artistic talent. Also, on our trip, I do hope to encounter a guitar I can briefly get my hands on, so I thought it would be nice for her to hear me play before our trip.

Once Elizabeth showed up for the performance, she and I went outside and sat in a section next to the bouncing equipment that was erected for the students' enjoyment on the front lawn. When I started my second song, the bouncing college students all quieted down to listen. That third set was definitely my best, with my friend sitting next to me. She said that she was AMAZED that I could sing and play the way that I did! I am so glad that I was able to share my songs with her.

Yet, I was so nervous that I was shaking a little, even while playing and singing, but I did okay — not perfect, of course, but okay. What a joy it is to experience such sweet success!

Wednesday, May 7, 2003: I had a wonderful dream last night. I dreamt of my adored, favorite grandmother, Grandma Marie, who passed over about thirty years ago. We were at my mother's house, and I talked with her and sat next to her at a family dinner. She was very old, yet lively and energetic and mentally alert, just as she had been in real life.

The day I depart for France (ten days from now), my husband, Tomas, will be attending the university graduation ceremony in my stead, together with my good friend, June, and her husband. Tomas will walk up and accept the diploma, and it has been making me sad that no one will be in the audience for him. He said he prefers it that way, as he is nervous enough about doing this. I know what he means, as I was vastly relieved when my music teacher this semester was unable to attend my mandatory public recital. It somewhat reduced the stress and internal pressure that I felt.

In the dream, I asked Grandma if she would mind attending the graduation, to be there for my husband, and she said that she would be glad to. She gave me the nicest, warmest hug, just like she always did in real life. I awoke worrying that Tomas would be angry that someone was coming to the graduation since he'd said he didn't want anyone. As soon as I was awakened enough to realize that it was a dream, I immediately tried to return to the dream state, to visit with my beloved Grandma again. I have often tried to visit her in my dreams but never with any success until now.

I love and miss my Grandma so very much. I have read that when we pass, we are greeted by those who in this life loved us the most dearly. I have little doubt that for me, it will be her. I choose to believe that she will indeed be there at the graduation, proud and happy, watching over Tomas, and that I need not worry about this most important ceremony. Interesting how those who love us the most ARE there for us, when we need them, is it not? I choose to believe that love does survive even "death."

I often rue that the English word for passing over is named death. If they had named it passage or transition or something else that acknowledges that it is a movement of the spirit from one state to another, perhaps humans would have, and would have historically had, a much different existence, with little or no fear of the passage. I wonder if some languages and cultures refer to it differently than English does.

May 11, 2003: This Mother's Day is the first one since Jack left home, more than six years ago, that I got to see him on Mother's Day. He brought a loving card and beautiful, dark purple flowers and stayed and visited for hours. Tomas, Jack, and I enjoyed our leftover turkey dinner. It blossomed into a relaxed and comfortable visit. I also played a few songs on the guitar for him. I mustered the courage, and he actually applauded!

Earlier in the day, Karen and Rick and Rick's friend had stopped over to get the $100 that Tomas and I are giving Karen to help her fly down to Florida to care for Mother after Mother's operation. I played my guitar and sang for them. What a satisfying moment it was when I hit that high note in John Hartman's "Gentle on My Mind" and Karen broke out in sincere applause, together with Rick and the others.

She is taking me to the airport on Saturday to go to France with the Penn State University group led by two professors. I'm lucky to have good friends, I know. It feels like such success just to have the courage to play for people and unbelievable success that they have sincerely enjoyed my music. It was so sweet, having company today.

Yesterday, our dinner with my college friend who had given me the turtle, June, and her husband Sam went fabulously. The food, as she later commented, was so delicious that it was "decadent" and we had fun and laughed together. It was especially satisfying that they so enjoyed the meal and the party. When she left, June hugged me about three times. I know she will really miss me while I'm in France. I am so amazed to have such good friends since not too long ago, Tomas and I actually didn't have any except for each other.

May 13, 2003: I dreamt of Jack's wife, Deborah, last night. I was in an outside place, sort of like the old County Fair and many other people were there. It was also like an outdoor picnic, a family type thing too. Anyway, it surprised me that Deborah was there, abruptly, and I greeted her and told her, looking her directly in the eyes, that I meant every word of the card that I sent her. I told her that I really appreciated the joy and happiness that she had brought into Jack's life and that I appreciate how much she loves him. (I, of course, didn't and wouldn't tell her that, the truth of the matter is, it is a wonder that any woman is willing to marry into this family with its unhealthy family history.)

In the dream, she saw that I was sincere, and her negativity melted away and she let me hug her. Then, as we continued to converse, I could see the depth of the beauty in her.

She had a shine and an inner goodness to her.

I was able, at long last, to see why Jack loved her. I awoke feeling wonderful and shared the dream with Tomas. What was his reply? The only way that he could envision her melting, he said, is like the wicked witch melting at the end of *The Wizard of Oz*.

I am nonetheless so grateful for that dream. I have long held onto the belief that there must be sides of Deborah that we have not yet seen. Otherwise, Jack would not have married her. If and when I encounter her again, this is what I will do. I will tell her that I really meant what I wrote, looking her straight in the eye so that she will know that I am sincere.

May 16, 2003: Tomorrow, I will realize two major life dreams, graduation from college and embarking on a journey to France. There I can, at long last, find out if I can speak French with the French, visit the Eiffel Tower, enjoy French cuisine, tour genuine castles, and see the beaches of Normandy! My excitement has been almost too much to bear!

There's no time to write more than this brief note today. *Il y a tellement de choses à faire!* (There is much to do!)

Chapter 16

STILL A PREDATOR

It started off as a happy, festive occasion. My sister, Jackie, and her third husband, David, were visiting. As always, I loved getting to spend some time with her. Of course, they stayed at Mother's house where, at the time, I was still residing.

On this particular day, Carl Stephens had come to visit and, since he was sober, was allowed to enter my mother's and adopted dad's home. Carl seemed a bit edgy but was putting on his best manners for my handsome brother-in-law and for my parents. At one point, David and Mother and Dad were in the kitchen, leaving Jackie and Carl alone in the living room and me in the adjoining room where I alone had full view of them and could hear their conversation.

Jackie was standing in front of the mantel, looking at me when our birth father approached her and began engaging her in conversation. As I watched in horror, I saw him quickly pounce on her, grabbing her roughly by the neck with his right hand and violently threatening her. With her neck greatly stretched, and her head tilted back, I was afraid to move or utter a sound. My shock deepened due to the fact that others stood so close by, within screaming distance, and yet, this heinous act still unfolded as he threatened:

"So, you think you're safe now because you have your husband here, in the kitchen, do you? If you scream, I can snap your neck in one second, long before anyone could come and help you! And don't think that I won't!"

I so wanted to scream, as I had sorely wanted to scream so many times in our childhood when I alone had been witness to so many horrors. Once again, as back then, abject terror froze my entire being from the bottom of my soul to the top of my useless head. Unable to speak, unable to move, utterly powerless against this evil, I watched, fearing any movements or sounds on my part might somehow make things worse for my sister, causing him to do it, to snap her neck and kill her.

Though I froze, Jackie certainly did not. To my amazement, my beloved sister showed no fear and responded as though she actually felt none. Although she was barely able to speak, her voice hinted more at disgust than fear as she boldly spoke. With her throat choked so tightly, she barely managed to squeak out the words, "Alright. You've had your fun. Now, let me go."

His failure to terrorize her somehow defeated him and he crumpled, removing his hand from its vice-like grip on her neck. She stepped away quickly, her hand to her neck, trying to massage away the injury.

I still hadn't moved, in shock that this could happen after all these years with no one coming to her rescue, as had always time and time again been the case in our youth. I watched as Jackie bolted out to the kitchen to tell David exactly what had happened. But he didn't believe her and stated that surely, she was overreacting. I had followed her in and asserted that no, she wasn't overreacting and that I had seen it. We two somehow could not convey the severity of his attack, however, and no one shared our horror.

In the end, Carl Stephens was chastised by Dad and asked to leave our home for "upsetting" us sisters. He feigned regret and offered apologies to my sister, saying he was sorry if his "kidding around" had bothered her in any way. And so, he left, having once again gotten away with terrorizing both my older sister and me, even while others were within earshot. Jackie and I were brutally reminded of what a monster he could truly be!!

Chapter 17

BROKEN PEOPLE

Curiosity — I wanted to learn something. I had always tried to analyze people, to figure them out, to understand the hows and whys, so that I could help them out of their nightmares. That is why, when I turned twenty-one, long before I was married, I decided to get drunk with my alcoholic father, the very same one who had tortured and terrorized me and my three sisters when we were too small to protect ourselves or to escape.

It was a day like any other summer day. The sun shone and the warm air relaxed and emboldened me. *I can handle this now,* I told myself. I was older, capable. I was as calm as the wind that day and fully determined.

He picked me up in his smoke-filled, dirty, old brown Ford and we drove to the seediest part of the area, the North Side, where he had "friends."

We entered their dingy, dilapidated apartment through a narrow alleyway, into a place that was nestled back and hidden from the world, entering first into their kitchen. I never saw any more of that apartment, just that kitchen with its bare floors and L-shaped counters with a small double sink and well-worn cabinets. A large, square table and chairs stood in the center of the room, with no tablecloth and no centerpiece.

They invited me to sit. Not wanting to go any farther into this possibly bug-infested hovel, I chose the chair closest to the door and sat down. Father took the chair across from me and the middle-aged, white-haired man and woman (possibly husband and wife) also sat opposite each other.

There was the "Hi, how are you?" chit chat, and after my father assured these two that he would soon have the money that he owed them, drinks were offered and then poured.

My drink of choice in those days was a rum and coke, and they were able to accommodate me. I sipped, careful not to get too tipsy. I didn't contribute much to the conversation except to answer the usual questions that middle-aged people would often ask of the young: Where do you work? How old are you? Are you in school? What do you want to do with your life?

The last question I couldn't answer, but on this day, I was a scientist of sorts, on a fact-finding expedition, trying to understand how to help a life-long alcoholic by entering his world in full. We drank. I had early on realized that these people were not exactly close friends of my father, but it struck me as odd that they accepted me so readily, sitting there with them, imbibing with these apparently habitual drinking buddies. And so, I kept quiet and listened more than I spoke.

Father did most of the talking, with the other two nodding or interrupting from time to time. It was clear that they didn't have much to say. He wasn't limiting his alcohol intake and soon became what I think of as sloppy drunk.

At some point, he began talking about growing up and how rough he had had it. He mentioned that, at one point in his teenage life, he and his parents had been forced to live in a one-room apartment, with a tiny stove in one corner for cooking, a small table and three chairs. In the opposite corner, a bed and a dresser for all of their belongings crowded together. A third corner held his tiny, uncomfortable bed. Once in a while, at night, after the lights went out, he could hear his parents' movements in the other bed, his dad's roughness, and his moans of pleasure. Quietly, Father said, he'd finally drift off to sleep, but not without disgust.

He began talking about me and my three sisters. He told his buddies how stunningly beautiful we had been as little girls, with our long, thick hair, big eyes, and slender legs. We were the three most beautiful girls ever to walk on this earth. He broke into tears as he described my oldest sister, Jackie, with her gorgeous bluest of eyes, her long, black eyelashes, her sweet voice, loving heart, and cascading dark chocolate brown hair. A tomboy, she possessed spunk and passion and often displayed fearlessness and a fierce protectiveness of others, starting at a very young age.

Then, he sobbed out the words, "And – God help me!! I wanted more than anything to sleep with her! God Forgive Me!"

Although I had already known that both of my older sisters had been abused by my father (fondling and slobbering over them when he was dead drunk), his words and sobbing struck me like a bolt of lightning, shocking me!

I glanced at his two other drinking buddies for a reaction to this dastardly confession, but incredibly, there was none. They sat there like two cardboard people, staring ahead as if they'd not heard, neither talking nor looking up, nor revealing any emotion whatsoever.

My father sat there sobbing loudly, and I realized — he was and had been for a long, long time, utterly broken. He couldn't help what he thought and felt. I also saw that he knew. He knew what an evil aberration this was, and he hated himself for it. He knew what he had done to his beautiful girls, and he couldn't live with it. And so, he drank. He regretted it to the depths of his soul.

The nightmare that was my father sat across

the table from me, sobbing, and with his confession made, now silent. Without a word, I managed to get myself out of that chair and ran out the door that I had instinctively sat closest to, escaping as fast as I could. I ran until I was out of breath and then found the nearest bus stop and waited. Still shocked and slightly tipsy, I waited for the next bus and with relief, boarded it quickly. Still stunned, I managed to find my way home.

I told no one until now what I had done, for I felt ashamed and horrified and stupid that I'd thought there was something to be gained. Yes, I had come to realize that he knew what he had done and, more importantly, he knew how abhorrently evil it all was. But no, I couldn't handle it. I wasn't ready. Still, I had learned something about my birth father. But it would take many decades for me to brave sharing this experience with others by writing these words.

Chapter 18

CLOSURE

Broken People CAN Heal —
Ideally, Through Other Broken People

My father had periods of sobriety during his adult life but never overcame his drastic, self-inflicted battle with the bottle. More tragically, in the end, my siblings and I also suffered terribly from addictions. I somehow found my way to healthy addictions as I eventually found and married my right somebody to love. He was another person broken in his own way. And somehow, we managed to heal each other's deep wounds — as much as they could be healed — and chose healthier additions such as exercise, endorphins, laughter and love.

Today, we cycle and swim and laugh and work and play together. Miraculously, together, we have built a healthy and joyful life for ourselves. I sensed early on in our relationship that we were fated to be married.

Later on, I realized that only because our wounds and "kinks" fit were we able to understand, love, and eventually heal ourselves and each other. Today, one of our goals is to be a bonus in the lives of other people. Together with our next-door neighbors who are more like family than friends, we plant and grow a humble, organic garden bursting with delicious veggies that we enjoy sharing with neighbors, friends and family. We like to believe that we have helped each other grow into healthy, loving and deeply grateful individuals, mostly unencumbered by those ghosts of the past.

Author Bio

The author, who wishes to remain anonymous, earned her B.S. in Information Sciences and Technology from Penn State University. A previous MENSA member, she received The Pennsylvania State University Academic Excellence Award and was also the grateful recipient of four scholarship awards.

Her story stands as a testament that healing from childhood sexual abuse is not only possible but transformative. It offers hope, validation, and inspiration to survivors everywhere—showing that no matter how deep the wounds, the human spirit has an infinite capacity to rise, to love, and to create a beautiful life of joy, purpose, and freedom.

She worked as a Network Administrator/Legal Assistant at various law firms. She enjoyed having three ideas published in the *WordPerfect for Law Office* periodical in the 1990s.

After retirement, she volunteered at The Literacy Society to help students earn their diplomas. She also volunteered as a Mah Jongg instructor and started a community Mah Jongg group in her local library.

She has entertained others by singing and playing guitar on stage more than once.

The author and her husband continue to enjoy each other, bicycling, swimming, laughing at themselves and each other, and any type of game. Together with the next-door neighbors, they sow and tend a summer organic vegetable garden that nurtures themselves, friends, family members, and others. Growing old together, they remain deeply grateful.